2ND EDITION

DAY TRADING

FROM UNDERSTANDING **RISK MANAGEMENT** AND
CREATING **TRADE PLANS** TO RECOGNIZING **MARKET**
PATTERNS AND USING **AUTOMATED SOFTWARE**,
AN ESSENTIAL PRIMER IN **MODERN DAY TRADING**

101

JOE DUARTE, MD

ADAMS MEDIA

NEW YORK   LONDON   TORONTO   SYDNEY   NEW DELHI

For my wonderful wife, Lourdes, who always puts up with me while I write books. And to all the readers and traders, without whose support I wouldn't be able to keep doing what I love. You're the music. I'm just the band.

Adams Media
An Imprint of Simon & Schuster, LLC
100 Technology Center Drive
Stoughton, Massachusetts 02072

Copyright © 2018, 2024 by
Simon & Schuster, LLC.

This Adams Media hardcover edition
October 2024
First Adams Media hardcover edition
January 2018

ADAMS MEDIA and colophon are registered
trademarks of Simon & Schuster, LLC.

Simon & Schuster: Celebrating 100 Years of
Publishing in 2024

For information about special discounts
for bulk purchases, please contact Simon &
Schuster Special Sales at 1-866-506-1949 or
business@simonandschuster.com.

The Simon & Schuster Speakers Bureau can
bring authors to your live event. For more
information or to book an event, contact the
Simon & Schuster Speakers Bureau at 1-866-
248-3049 or visit our website at
www.simonspeakers.com.

Manufactured in the United States of America

1 2024

Library of Congress Cataloging-in-Publication
Data
Names: Duarte, Joe, author. | Borman, David.
Day trading 101.
Title: Day trading 101, 2nd edition / Joe Duarte,
MD.
Description: 2nd edition. | Stoughton,
Massachusetts: Adams Media, [2024] | Series:
Adams 101 series | Includes index.
Identifiers: LCCN 2024015270 | ISBN
9781507222362 (hc) | ISBN 9781507222379
(ebook)
Subjects: LCSH: Day trading (Securities) |
Electronic trading of securities.
Classification: LCC HG4515.95 .D83 2024 |
DDC 332.64/20285--dc23/eng/20240405
LC record available at https://lccn.loc
.gov/2024015270

ISBN 978-1-5072-2236-2
ISBN 978-1-5072-2237-9 (ebook)

Contains material adapted from the following
title published by Adams Media, an Imprint
of Simon & Schuster, LLC: *Day Trading 101*
by David Borman, copyright © 2018, ISBN
978-1-5072-0581-5.

CONTENTS

INTRODUCTION

If you've ever wanted to know how to make more money in the lucrative world of day trading, this book sets you up for success. From learning your current competition in the market to understanding how COVID-19 impacted commodities to realizing what it takes to get higher returns in today's economic world, there's no doubt that day trading is a complicated but rewarding way to make some additional income. Each day, more and more people are curious about how they can succeed with this exciting side hustle.

In *Day Trading 101, 2nd Edition*, you get access to the most up-to-date information regarding how to invest in the stock market at peak times so you can earn money quickly. You'll learn that day traders buy and sell stocks many times in a single day and how to capture gains and book profits on your trades during the hours the markets are open. Throughout this book, you'll learn more about what's involved in the world of investment opportunities, including:

- How AI, algorithms, and high frequency trading are impacting market pricing
- What cryptocurrency means for day trading
- How you can use the Federal Reserve as an indicator to plan your day
- The differences in trading seasonally (and what that means for the gold market)

- How to use interest rates and liquidity to understand the big picture
- And more!

This book will walk you through the basic concepts of how to start day trading, from opening and funding your trading account, looking for profitable trades, knowing when to exit a trade for a good amount of profit, and steering clear of bad trades. You will learn the differences between day trading, short-term trading, and investing, and you will see what you'll need to get up and running in your day trading account to make your trading manageable, enjoyable, and profitable. All it takes is a bit of knowledge, insight, discipline, and flexibility. With a little time and practice, you'll be able to read the market's signals, determine the good trades from the bad trades, and start booking profits.

Whichever stocks you focus on, or where you start your day trading journey, *Day Trading 101, 2nd Edition*, will assist you in your goal to learn more about this fast-paced, fun economic opportunity. So, let's begin.

Chapter 1

Introduction to Markets and Trading

Trading, day trading, and investing are terms that are used to describe the buying and selling of financial products, which for all intents and purposes are traded electronically. Whether they're trading stocks, commodities such as oil or gold, or foreign currency, day traders and traders use computers to buy and sell in the financial markets. Most people are familiar with the US markets such as the stock market, but the financial markets are worldwide, and it is possible to trade stocks issued by European companies, gold warehoused in Asia, or the currencies of developing nations. What ties them all together is that the trading is done electronically and can be done from your home computer or, in many cases, from your tablet or smartphone.

WHAT IS DAY TRADING?

Your New Side Hustle and Many Options for Day Trading

The COVID-19 pandemic changed everything. And after the dust began to settle, it became evident that many people needed a second job, a side hustle, or sometimes both. Day trading can fill those needs by providing extra income while potentially becoming the primary way to pay bills and lead the best life possible.

When people hear the word "trading," they usually think of the stock market and 401(k) plans (or other retirement accounts). But that's not really stock trading; it's investing. People who trade stocks don't deposit money into a 401(k) or brokerage account with each payroll check. Instead, they buy and sell stocks to make a profit.

Many traders think long term and buy and hold stocks for a certain length of time—sometimes years. But there's another kind of trading: day trading. Day traders buy and sell stock within a twenty-four-hour period. Sometimes they hold the stock for only minutes, sometimes for a few hours. Day trading is the process of starting a trading session at the beginning of the day in 100% cash, buying and selling securities during the day for profits, and making sure to sell off all the account holdings by the end of the day, thereby returning to all cash at the end of the trading session.

Day traders buy and sell stocks many times in a single day. Their goal is to capture gains and book profits on their trades during the hours the markets are open. They repeat the process of starting in cash, trading, booking profits, and ending the day in cash every day. Although the profit on each trade is often relatively small, the volume of their trades allows day traders to book huge profits on average-sized accounts over the year. As the profits come in, the trader's account grows in value, allowing larger trades.

Another distinguishing feature of day trading is the use of "leverage" to amplify purchasing power. When day traders use leverage (also called margin accounts) in their trading strategies, they are essentially buying stock or securities with credit. This is much like purchasing a house with only a 10% or 20% down payment and a mortgage for the balance. In the case of day trading, the trader puts up cash or other securities for the down payment, and the brokerage account lends him money to buy more stock or other securities. This means that with the right management, relatively small accounts can book sizable profits.

Finally, day trading is enhanced via the availability of twenty-four-hour markets. Day trading can be done whenever the markets are open: for stocks, this usually means 9:30 a.m. to 4:00 p.m. Eastern US time, as well as during the pre-market and after hours sessions, which run from 4:00 a.m. to 9:30 a.m. and 4:00 p.m. to 8:00 p.m. But while the US stock market is only open during the day, other markets are open twenty-four hours a day, six days a week. This means you can keep your day job while building up your skills at trading during your off hours. You can trade on your own time. You can even trade on a smartphone or a tablet; brokerage houses offer sophisticated trading platforms for both.

Trading can be done anywhere with Internet access and it doesn't need to take a lot of time. You might spend only an hour a day looking for trades and only trade two to four times a week. It's up to you how you want to build your trading business.

Start a Process Checklist

Write down the needed steps in a checklist to develop your day trading career and check them off one by one as you master each step. The easy way is to follow the guidelines set in this book. First, learn about the markets, and the rest will follow.

FUNCTIONS OF THE MARKETS

Market Makers and Market Pricing

The market is a complex entity because of the interactions that take place between financial traders and investors, who use products and platforms to buy and sell assets. The traders' actions are facilitated by intermediaries (exchanges and market makers), and these traders' actions are guided by rules crafted and enforced by governments and independent agencies. Through these interconnected means, professional and personal traders and investors carry out both short-term and long-term trades and investments in financial products such as stocks, foreign monies, and commodities such as gold and oil. Together, traders, investors, exchanges, and rule crafters and enforcers come together to form the market, a term which refers to both the industry and the collective mechanism as a whole, not just stocks, bonds, or other traded instruments.

Say the word "markets," and most people think of the tumultuous "pits" that we often see on television and in pictures of the New York Stock Exchange (NYSE). Dozens of traders are closely gathered, waving their hands wildly while yelling out buy and sell orders. These "pits" are on the floor of the stock exchanges, and are highly symbolic in the days of electronic trading. In the past, the trading pits were places where you could find independent traders and market makers. In the twenty-first century, you're most likely to trade against a machine because the market's backbone now is mostly composed of servers housed in climate-controlled data centers.

MARKET MAKERS

Market makers are intermediaries, traders who match buyers with sellers. They make money by buying and selling all available stock in which they are dealers. They are the first to buy and sell all orders coming through the exchange floor for that stock, and they earn a commission on each trade. The downside of this is that if the market has a bad day, they still have to buy all shares of their specialty stock, whatever the price. This is true even if their order book is full and they have very few buyers. Market makers facilitate the efficient and orderly operation of the investment markets in good times and bad.

Because market makers (the middle men who connect buyers and sellers) have access to the market's trend before anyone else, they legally buy or sell shares for their own account before anyone else does. This gives them an advantage in making profits, while being perfectly legal and preserving their ability to remain solvent. Without market makers the financial markets would likely be chaotic.

Many market makers work for large firms such as Morgan Stanley or Merrill Lynch; others are employed by private account holders who own a "seat" on the exchange. Having a seat allows them to put a person on the floor of the exchange to get in on the trading action.

Trades are often made in bulk orders of one thousand shares or more, but floor traders and machine traders can handle smaller trades (hundred-share lots or even smaller). Human and mechanical traders trade for their own account or for firms that buy shares for their client's accounts. In either case, the motivation of market makers is the access to all trades that come through the floor and a commission on each trade that they handle for clients, as well as profiting for their own account. Market makers are strictly regulated by the Securities and Exchange Commission (SEC), the Financial

Industry Regulatory Authority (FINRA), and the National Futures Association (NFA). The SEC is the government body that polices, investigates, and prosecutes financial and market fraud in the United States. FINRA and NFA are self-governing industry watchdogs that monitor and regulate all US-based stock, foreign exchange market, and futures professionals.

Fiduciary Care

While market makers are a form of broker, only FINRA/NFA brokers registered to provide "care of custodial control of client accounts" are required to provide a fiduciary service: meaning only these registered brokers are required to put their client's financial needs above their own.

Determining Price

In addition to providing a physical or electronic gathering place for buyers and sellers of financial products such as stocks, foreign currency, and futures, the world's marketplaces help buyers and sellers determine the current price of what's being traded. Trading screens scattered throughout the trading floor of the exchanges show a buy and a sell price for each stock. This price data is transferred to the data feed you see on your computer screen. The prices are updated constantly so that traders can see what a trade is worth moment to moment, allowing them what is called price discovery. The buy prices are a bit higher than the sell prices; the difference between the buy/sell is called bid/ask spread.

If you are selling a stock, you'll get the bid price; if you are buying a stock, you'll get the ask price. If you're buying a stock, it will cost more than you would get if you had the same stock and you were selling. The difference between the two prices, the spread, is pocketed by the dealers and floor brokers as their profit for the service of being market makers. Financial products that are traded in massive quantities daily usually have a tight spread: the difference between the buying and selling price is very small, or tight.

For example, if you were to buy one hundred shares of Apple stock (AAPL) at $101.50 per share and instantly sold all one hundred of those AAPL shares, your sales price would be about $101.40. You would instantly lose ten cents per share, for a total loss of $10 on the trade. This difference in price is the amount that the dealer or floor broker makes on the trade. Remember, the floor brokers make money with every buy and sell order that comes across their order book—it doesn't matter if you lost money on the trade. Each trading day, there are thousands of buy and sell orders, and the floor brokers earn a small sliver of profit on each trade they handle for their clients.

The volume at which shares or other financial products are traded is referred to as their liquidity. The more liquid a product is (i.e., the more often it is traded), the smaller the spread. The more illiquid a product is (i.e., the less it is traded), the wider the spread.

Bid/Ask Spreads Vary Widely

Spreads can vary widely between traded products: the spread of an electronically traded futures contract for 100 ounces of gold could be as little as $10. At the same time, the spread of 100 ounces of actual gold bullion from a reputable precious metals dealer could be as high as $30 per ounce, or $3,000.

PRIMARY AND SECONDARY MARKETS

Two other terms you'll hear as you learn more about trading are primary market and secondary market. The primary market is where new stocks and bonds are first made available for public purchase. When a company is raising cash for operations for the first time, investors can pay cash for an equity ownership stake in the company, which is embodied in shares of stock. In return, the owners of the company give up a percentage of control of their company to the investors. The company then takes the cash and uses the money to grow further. This initial sale of stock is called an initial public offering, or IPO.

Once the stock has been sold, it becomes a part of the secondary market, where it can be traded among investors and day traders. Most times this is done through a brokerage account or an online trading platform. As a day trader, the financial products you will be trading will all be offered on the secondary market—you will be day trading by buying and selling on the exchanges through your brokerage trading platform. Your trading platform will differ depending upon the product you trade, whether it's stocks, foreign exchange, or futures. Not only are these different products, but each brokerage firm will offer its own. The basics will all be the same though: order entry, notations as to available purchasing limits, and each gain and/or loss of every trade. The displays range from the very simple to the complex.

The money paid for a trade is given to the previous owner of the stock, and the purchasing trader receives the stock. The company that originally issued the stock never receives any money from the secondary market. The only time the company receives the money from the sale of stock is when it's initially sold on the primary market. From then on, traders and investors buy and sell stock from their own accounts, and only to each other.

WHO'S WHO IN THE MARKETPLACE

Banks, Hedge Funds, CTAs, HFTs, and Trading Houses

Before you start searching the market, looking for trades, and living the often thrilling life of a day trader, it's best to know a little about the institutions that are integral to the world's stock, currency, and commodities markets. Aside from brokerage and market making services, all of the institutions within this chapter also trade for their own accounts and rely on one characteristic when they trade: algorithmic/mechanical trading programs (algos).

INVESTMENT BANKS

Within the world's marketplace of stocks, bonds, mutual funds, futures, and currency, there are a few key players. The first of these is the investment banks. These are at the top of the food chain in the trading business (think Goldman Sachs, Morgan Stanley, UBS, and J.P. Morgan). This is because when companies are raising capital for the first time, it is the investment banks that write and prepare the documents, provide advice, and help "place" the initial run of stock that the company will offer. ("Place" in this context means the very first listing of the stock on the stock exchange ever, thereafter available to the public to buy in their trading accounts for investment or trading.) As discussed earlier, if the company is raising capital on the stock exchange for the first time, the first shares of stock sold to the public are called an IPO, or initial public offering. These IPOs are very complex. The company will hire an investment bank to determine how many shares will be sold, at what price they sell, and if any other legal contracts will be tied to the shares. The bank will then use its vast connections in the investment world to find buyers of the stock at the initial price. This is the price it will sell at when the company goes public.

Investment banks have first dibs on the stock and will sell large blocks to their best customers. Regular traders can own shares of the new stock after it has debuted on the exchange and is therefore trading live.

HEDGE FUNDS

The second group of players in the markets is hedge funds. These are privately owned trading houses that invest both their owners' monies and their customers' monies at highly leveraged amounts. Not only are hedge funds highly leveraged pools of investment money, but they also use several trading styles. These styles range from higher-level views of the world's trading environments (such as Global Macro funds), which trade any financial product with a "no restraints" policy on where gains can be captured, to derivative-only funds (managed futures funds) that are designed to make money when stocks go up or down in value (long/short funds), or even special situations funds (leveraged buyouts, or distressed asset funds, which only buy stocks in companies that are undergoing trauma: management takeovers, bankruptcies, fiscal trouble, etc.).

Within the umbrella of hedge funds are Commodity Trading Advisors and High Frequency Traders, which have different roles in the market. These are the professional institutional traders who are traditionally described as providers of liquidity for the market. That's only part of the story, as they are also the adversaries of individual traders.

Commodity Trading Advisors (CTAs)

Some hedge funds operate as Commodity Trading Advisors (CTAs). They specialize in algorithmic/mechanical trading programs (algos), whose strategies are based on technical analysis of key price areas on price charts. Distilled, their trading method refers to a simple principle central to algo trading known as "if this happens, do this."

For example, a CTA trading program may be designed to respond to a specific economic report and the market's response to the report, such as the monthly US payroll data. The program may be instructed to buy or sell based on the number of new jobs created and how the bond market and the S&P 500 index (SPX) respond to the number. Because CTAs are large investors, their actions are usually big market influencers, creating day trading opportunities.

High Frequency Traders (HFTs)

Similar to CTAs, High Frequency Traders (HFTs) operate algo trading programs. HFTs buy space at the data centers where the exchange computers are housed. The proximity of their servers to those of the exchange's primary data gives them access to the order flow from trades before the public. They are the second entities to see whether the majority of trades are to buy or sell stock. HFT computers are programmed to follow the primary order flow. When buyers overwhelm sellers, HFT computers buy stock aggressively. When sellers overwhelm buyers, HFT computers sell stock.

Hedge Funds Are Less Invincible Than in the Past

In the days prior to the 2007–2008 subprime mortgage crisis, hedge funds were seen as invincible investors: Their access to information and deep pockets gave them an outsized advantage. Those days are long gone. Social media disseminates information rapidly and automated trading leaves footprints on price charts, which day traders and other savvy investors can discern.

Market makers and hedge funds (like CTAs and HFTs) can be massive buyers and sellers in the markets. They all use both equity and derivative positions (also known as options and futures) to diversify their accounts and to manage risk of loss to a very sophisticated level. The combination of equity and derivative trades often increase the market's volatility. This is especially true during periods when major developments outside the market influence the trading scene. Hedge funds' algos help them to execute the trades faster.

Hedge funds are managed by the most sophisticated and powerful day traders and position traders in the world. They play often and spend large sums of money to hire the best algo programmers available. Hedge fund buying and selling can move the markets up or down, often in big ways. However, their effects have been lessened by the advent of social media and improved price chart analysis. People still take notice when a rumor of a large hedge fund making a trade is in the news, but these funds are not as influential as they once were.

Hedge Fund Performance

The major wealth management firms heavily recommend hedge funds of all investment styles. This is good news, as the money trails left by hedge funds on price charts can be excellent income sources for day traders. Some houses such as UBS and Morgan Stanley recommend that 15%–20% of an investment portfolio should be invested in alternative investments for proper diversification and risk/reward profile. Of this 15%–20%, hedge funds are included along with other forms of complex alternative investments, such as private equity and derivative funds.

Hedge fund performance has gone up and down over the years; traditionally, they did best when global markets were in turmoil. Now, this is not a reliable gauge. Instead, they do better when markets trend up or down for long periods. They are designed to offer maximum diversification to an overall investment portfolio and are built with layers of diversification. Yet, some of these safety measures (hedges) can backfire, creating opportunities for day traders. If the equity markets of the world are all doing well, especially when European, US, and Asian markets are doing well, then traders and investors will most likely earn more and do better with a unidirectional, nondiversified trading strategy. During sustained up trends, stocks will generally move in one direction most of the time. While there may be up-and-down days, on average the market will move in one direction over weeks and months (or even years!).

Simple trading strategies work the best to deliver profits. Unidirectional and nondiversified, long-only equities, options, or equity futures can be the best and highest performing trading strategies. Keep it simple! Buy low, sell high. If the market seems to go up every day, then go long only (buy low and sell higher). This is easy to understand and simple to set up on your trading platform. In addition, simple long-only trades are cheaper to execute than diversified trades due to commission costs.

Hedges Can Backfire

The term "hedge" defines an investment strategy designed to manage risk. A common hedge is that of buying put options (which rise in price when the underlying asset being hedged falls in price). Put options can be very useful in the early stages of a market decline, but when the majority of investors decides to buy put options, it's often a prelude to a market bottom. The CBOE Put/Call Ratio is a useful indicator through which these periods can be identified.

PROFESSIONAL TRADING HOUSES

Another group of investors (aside from independent traders) is professional trading houses, such as mutual funds and investment companies. Mutual funds are pools of monies that are professionally managed by fund managers. These investment vehicles are generally long-only equity or bond funds.

If you have a 401(k) at work, you are most likely investing in professionally managed mutual funds offered by mutual fund families. These mutual fund families offer customers professionally managed investments with smaller minimums and excellent diversification. Mutual funds pool their customers' investments. They then take the money and buy stocks or bonds (or both). Mutual funds can hold ten, fifty, or a hundred or more different equity positions. The managers will then buy and sell, capturing short-term gains for their shareholders. Shareholders will also capture gains on stocks or bonds that go up in value in the market, even if they haven't been sold yet (these are referred to as unrealized gains). Investment companies such as mutual fund families are one of the largest buyers of equities and bonds in the marketplace due to the vast number of investors—especially retirees—using them.

COMMONLY TRADED PRODUCTS

Stocks and Leveraged Exchange-Traded Funds (ETFs)

Before you begin day trading, you'll need to know some of the different investment products that can be traded. Some of them are easier to understand and set up as trades but offer less potential for return. Other products require a more complex trade setup and may offer more potential to trade at higher returns while sometimes carrying higher risks.

TRADING STOCKS

The most basic type of day trading is trading equities also known as stocks. This is because the basic concept underlying this type of trading—i.e., buy low and sell high—is easy to understand, and online trading platforms such as E-Trade, Merrill Edge, and Scottrade make it simple. Stock trading works well when the world's stock markets are generally going up in value.

Go Long, Go Short

If you buy a stock expecting that its price will rise, you're taking a long position. If you sell a stock in the expectation that its price will fall and you'll be able to buy it back at a lower price, you're taking a short position, or shorting the stock. You can also go long via buying a call option, while going short via buying a put option.

Equity Order Entry

When you're day trading stock, you sign in to your trading platform and type in the symbol of the stock (such as Apple Inc., with a symbol of AAPL). Your trading platform will show the current price of one share, along with the maximum number of shares you can afford to buy with the money currently in your account.

The next step is to enter the number of shares (say, ten shares), and then click the "buy now" button. Instantly, your trade is entered. You now own ten shares of Apple. If one share of Apple is selling at $100 per share, your total cost of the ten shares is $1,000 ($100/share × 10 shares). The trade has a small additional cost, usually under $10 (in this case, most likely around $5). Your trading platform now shows that you own ten shares of AAPL, with a true cost of $1,005.

Stock Symbols

The website *MarketWatch* (www.marketwatch.com) has a handy service that allows you to look up stock symbols. Just type in the name of the company and you'll find the stock symbol, the current price of the stock, its previous closing price, and other helpful information.

Monitoring Profits

If Apple stock goes up in value, the trading platform will show your trade value moving from $1,005 to a higher figure as each share gains value. If, as the minutes and hours tick by, the price of AAPL goes from $100 per share to $102.50 per share, your AAPL trade will show a value of $1,025 ($102.50 × 10 shares). Because you've spent $5 to buy the shares of Apple, the trading platform will show the net profit of the trade at $20. As you can see, in one day your trade has turned a $20 profit, or made a 2% return for the day.

As noted earlier, day traders close their trades at the end of the day. If they do their job well, they realize a profit and end the day with cash in hand. Closing out your trade will cost you an additional trading fee, typically a flat rate of around $5 for this type of trade. If the Apple trade was the only one you made during the day, this would leave you with a $15 profit. While this $15/trade seems small, it is a trade with very little risk or effort. You're in and out in a few minutes or hours, and your cash is back in your account, safe and sound.

If you made this or a similar trade just fifteen days a month, you'd net $225 in profits per month on your $1,000 trading account. This is 22.5% profit per month, or about 250% per year return on your $1,000 account. These types of trades are safe and manageable, and in this case your trading account would grow to $2,500 by the end of the year with very little effort.

As the amount of money in your account increases, you can also take on bigger trades, increasing your profit potential even more. This type of trading could easily and safely return 250%–375% on a $1,000 account.

LEVERAGED EXCHANGE-TRADED FUNDS

Now let's see what happens if you up your game and engage in more complex trading. This involves using leveraged exchange-traded funds (ETFs).

An ETF is a basket of multiple stocks that can be traded on the markets. An ETF trades at a specific dollar amount but contains fractional shares of twenty to fifty different stocks, each valued at a fraction of their current trading list price. An ETF's trading value is determined by adding up the dollar amount of the pooled assets and dividing that by the number of shares outstanding (that is, the shares available for traders to buy and sell). ETFs are favored by professional traders in part because of the benefits that come with diversification (the multiple company stocks contained within the fund), and because they are useful vehicles for trading with the dominant market trend. ETFs also often have massive trading volumes, which can result in significant daily gains. This makes them perfect for day trading.

Derivatives

Here's another useful term in this discussion: derivatives. If you were reading the papers during the 2008 financial crisis, you probably came across this word a lot. A derivative is a financial contract or asset whose price is determined by the price of something else. For instance, you want to buy a commodity—say, bushels of corn—as an investment, hoping that the price of corn will go up. But you don't want to store a thousand bushels of corn in your garage. You can instead buy a futures contract, which specifies that at some determined point to come, you'll take delivery of that corn. If the price of corn goes up, so will the price of the futures contract, which you can then sell to someone else for a profit. The futures contract is an example of a derivative. Nowadays, options are also derivatives and are more widely used by day traders than futures contracts.

Leveraged ETFs are the same as ETFs but they are financially engineered to use margins and derivatives in such a way to amplify the movement of the same base ETF by either two times (2x) or three times (3x) the gain. In other words, a base ETF might move up 1.5% during the trading day, while the 2x ETF would move up two times the same amount, or 3%. The same for the 3x ETF: it would move up 4.5%. It should be noted that while 2x and 3x ETFs offer higher gains, they're also riskier than ordinary ETFs.

Bull and Bear ETFs

Leveraged ETFs also come in "bull" and "bear" designs. A bear refers to a bear market (when the markets are falling) and a bull refers to a bull market (when the markets are rising). A bull 3x ETF would go up three times the percentage of a normal ETF, while a bear 3x ETF would make money when the unleveraged ETF goes down.

Bear ETFs can be complicated to use, but they do offer the day trader a simple method to set up trades that make money when the market is falling. The best way to use these is intraday, meaning they are traded within a single trading day during normal market hours and not set up before the market opens. As you will learn later, while trading in and out throughout one day, it is possible to program a trade before the markets officially open in the morning and still close out the trade before the end of the day. In this case, you wouldn't want to use bull and bear ETFs with preprogrammed trades. The key is to get in and out quickly: ride the 2x or 3x bear for profit and then sell to lock in your gains. Bear ETFs, especially leveraged ones, are risky, so you should be cautious and only use them to make a little extra profit in bad markets.

MORE COMMONLY TRADED PRODUCTS

Futures and Foreign Exchange Trading

Two other markets that lend themselves well to day trading are futures and currency trading (referred to as Forex), though they are a bit trickier to trade than stocks and ETFs. Futures contracts are easily shorted (which means the day trader will make money when the market goes down) and Forex trading relies on one currency going up or down against another currency in order for the trade to earn a profit.

FUTURES

A futures contract, in essence, is an agreement to buy or sell something in the future at an agreed-upon price. As discussed earlier, futures are part of the group of financial products called derivatives.

The exchanges determine the number of units and settlement date of futures contracts, and they can't be modified. This means that contracts are uniformly interchangeable, so trading is simplified. Each futures contract has a buyer and a seller. One of the parties involved in the trade is a hedger and one is a speculator. The hedger enters the contract to offset her risk that the future price of the product will move up or down against her.

For example, an airline expects the price of jet fuel will rise substantially in the next six months, and this price increase will make it difficult for the company to make a profit. The company's traders buy an oil futures contract with a set price for oil six months in the future to lock in the price of jet fuel for the company's fleet of airplanes, locking in a price the company can afford to pay for fuel and still make an acceptable profit. The contract is hedging the fuel expense risk to the company, managing the future expenses and profit of the company.

Hedgers and Speculators

A hedger is someone who uses the physical product he's buying or selling. He uses the futures trading contract to lock in his price and minimize his losses when he finally either buys or sells the commodity sometime in the future. Speculators are traders whose only goal is to make money based on the direction of a price trend. For example, in the futures market, speculators don't want delivery of the underlying commodity in which they invest, but they are willing to buy into the asset as long as it's rising. Indeed, day traders are the ultimate speculators.

On the other end of the oil futures contract is a speculator, who does not have an actual need for oil or jet fuel. Their expectation is that the price of oil will be less than the contract price in the next six months. Seeing an opportunity to make a profit, they buy the futures contract that the airline company manager is selling. The speculator makes money when the locked-in price of the contract is less than the actual price of the commodity—in this case, oil. So, if you buy a crude oil contract for one thousand barrels at $70 a barrel in July for oil to be delivered in November and the actual price of crude oil increases during that period, the value of your futures contract will also increase. If oil moves up to $90 per barrel by the time the contract expires, you own one thousand barrels of oil at $70 per barrel, which you can sell on the market for $90 per barrel, making a profit of $20,000 ($20 × 1,000 barrels). Futures contracts like these are bought and sold in huge quantities daily, creating a profitable market for day traders.

Standard & Poor's 500 Index

The Standard & Poor's 500 Index (S&P 500) is a market indicator based on five hundred of the largest companies listed on the New York Stock Exchange (NYSE). It's used as one of the key indicators for the overall health of the stock market.

Margin and Futures

Futures contracts offer a margin up to 50:1 (in other words, for every one unit of collateral you put up, you can borrow fifty times as much). This means if you used full margin on your futures account, you could theoretically amplify the gains of the S&P 500 Index of 1% up to fifty times more, or 50% gains. This is the maximum amount of the trading value of the account. To manage the risk in your account, you might only commit 20% of your total portfolio to the trade, meaning you would earn about 10% gain on the trade. To explain further, if you used 20% of your total portfolio at 50:1 margin, it would look like this: .20 × 50 = 10%. Therefore, you would earn 10% gain on each actual 1% gain made by the future.

The higher margin of futures amplifies your trades at a much higher rate than you could with stocks or ETF trades. The flip side is losses can mount faster. You can make much larger trades in a futures brokerage account than you can with a stock brokerage account. A $2,500 cash balance in a futures account allows for $125,000 worth of S&P 500 futures contracts, whereas a stock trading account with the same $2,500 cash balance only buys $3,750 worth of S&P 500 ETFs.

Futures contracts are more complex because the prices rise and fall rapidly and they require constant attention. Futures trading requires experience and will test you, as it takes skill to make trades at a 50:1 margin. The skills you'll learn in this book—reading the market, studying the news, tracking the world's economies, and looking for good trade setups—will be tested to the maximum with futures trading. It is not for the faint of heart, but it is where the professionals can earn a big living, often delivering 100% or more in profits monthly. Be aware that many futures traders find them quite difficult to master and close their accounts within a few years of struggling and racking up losses.

Move into futures after you've mastered the basics of day trading. Gold, oil, and the S&P 500 are the largest and easiest futures markets to master and trade in. They offer direct connections to the ETF and equity world, allowing for great on-the-job training. Agricultural futures contracts, such as corn and soybeans, are difficult to trade because their prices follow grain demands, weather, and international trading contracts, as opposed to strictly economic news.

S&P 500 Futures Contracts

With Standard & Poor's 500 (S&P 500) Index futures contracts, each contract acts as a dollar representation of the whole S&P 500 Index. If the S&P 500 Index lists a value of 2,575 points, a futures contract for the S&P 500 will trade at $2,575.

Day trading S&P 500 futures contracts allows you to participate in the fluctuations of the index (in which movements of 0.5% 1.5% daily are common) with more leverage than with an S&P 500 Index ETF. For example, if you trade the iShares Core S&P 500 ETF (symbol IVV), and you use a full 50% margin in your account, you could amplify a 1% gain in the index by an additional 50%, making it into a 1.5% gain.

CURRENCY TRADING

In currency trading, or Forex (foreign exchange) trading, the trader picks two currencies and decides which currency will gain in value against the other. If you go to Europe and exchange your US dollars for euros, you are, in a sense, going into the Forex market; you're "selling" US dollars (USD) and "buying" euros (EUR). If many people, traders, banks, and governments sell one currency and buy another, this pushes down the price of the sold currency and boosts the price of the bought currency. In the stock market, if everyone is selling AAPL, then the price will go down. The same principle of supply and demand applies to currency trading.

Currency Value

Besides supply and demand, a currency can rise or fall for several reasons. A reliable one is interest rates: When central banks raise interest rates, their country's currency generally rises. Other influential factors include inflation (which makes each unit of currency worth less) but can be countered by raising interest rates. Political instability, rising or declining productivity, and natural disasters are usually negative for individual currencies. Effectively day trading in the Forex market means learning about international political, social, and economic conditions.

Forex trading is easier than futures trading. While there are a variety of margins available—10:1, 20:1, 50:1—there are only a small handful of currency pairs that are available on most Forex trading platforms. From these, a day trader can master two or three currency pairs and do very well.

Trading the same two or three currency pairs over and over, day in and day out, can make a Forex trader an expert quickly. This expertise naturally leads to better and more successful trading, and therefore higher profits. You should consider currency trading as a way to have large, profitable trades (20:1 and 50:1 margin) that you can master in a relatively short time. Your account size can be small too—a $250-$500 cash balance in a Forex account is more than enough to get you started and make substantial profits quickly. It's normal to see $50-$75 daily profits in a $500 Forex account, and the trading can be done twenty-four hours a day, nearly six days a week. In short, for the day trader just starting out, Forex offers an excellent combination of trading power and easy mastery.

TRADING BASICS

Know Day Trading from the Ground Up

Most people who are in the stock market, bond market, or other type of investment are really investors, and not traders. What makes the difference between investing and trading in the market? The real answer is twofold: leverage and time of trade.

TRADERS

Most traders use leverage in their accounts, either by using margin accounts or trading leveraged investment vehicles (such as leveraged 2x or 3x ETFs or leveraged mutual funds). In either case, the account is designed to use the dollar balance of the account plus any invested assets as a down payment for a loan from the brokerage house to borrow more money and then invest more with this borrowed money.

For instance, a trader has a $5,000 balance in his account, consisting of cash, stock, or mutual funds. Based on this, the brokerage house will "lend" him more cash using the balance in the account as collateral for the "loan." The trader will then use a combination of his cash and his available loan to make purchases of securities beyond what he could have bought with his cash. Securities can be purchased in excess of 150%–175% of the cash balance of the account, depending upon the quality of the collateral.

If you are to use margin, then the higher the quality of your collateral, the higher the limit of additional margin the brokerage firm will allow. In the case of volatile stocks or leveraged ETFs, your brokerage firm might be limited to only 50% additional margin of your total account value. Higher-quality assets in the account always allow a higher level of margin, up to the amount specified by regulation.

In times of low market volatility and better economic times, government regulators allow the brokerage houses to increase the available margin, which offers traders the opportunity to take risks by making larger trades overall. The looser margin rules often come during an economic environment of low interest rates, the benefit of which is then passed on to the trader. Remember, the margin is a loan, and prevailing interest rates apply to the trader's margin— which in turn is a cost of trading and can eat into the profitably of the trade!

Margin Rates May Vary

Regulators set the margin leverage amounts available to traders according to the health of the markets: In good times, leverage could be as high as 90%, but in bad economic times they could drop to lower than 30%. Brokerages have the final say as to how much of the regulator-allowed margin they accept for each individual account.

INVESTORS

Investors usually have cash-only balances in their accounts. Many of these account holders have their retirement money invested in financial securities, either in their 401(k)s or in an IRA or a Roth IRA housed at a brokerage firm. The money is intended for use at some specific time in the future, and the date is usually known, since most people know more or less when they're going to retire. Investors put money in the account in a lump sum and then use it to buy securities, which they then hold for months or years. Alternatively, they could put cash into their account at timed intervals, such as when money is deducted from each payroll check, month after month, year after year, and placed in a retirement account such as a company 401(k).

Buy and Hold

The investor's philosophy is usually "buy and hold," meaning that the investment will see higher returns if the stock, bond, or mutual fund is not traded but rather held for extended periods. The idea is that the markets go up steadily over time and that there is no benefit to selling in short time frames.

Often, an investor will also reduce risk through a strategy called dollar cost averaging. This is the practice of putting the same amount of money into a chosen investment at set intervals, usually with each paycheck. This is the method that is used in payroll deduction for 401(k)s and often for self-directed IRAs. This approach works especially well with long-term investment goals such as retirement needs or children's college tuition funding programs. And if the market takes a sudden downturn, the entire fund is not impacted—just the part that's already invested.

TRADER VERSUS INVESTOR

In summary:

Traders
- Use leverage to amplify the gains of their trading accounts with added purchasing power through the use of margin

- Deploy their margin, which is actually a loan issued by the brokerage house, to purchase more stock
- Are in and out of a trade in a matter of minutes, hours, or days; occasionally, a trader will hold a position for a few weeks or a few months (called position trading)

Investors
- Almost exclusively use cash accounts with no leverage
- Only use the cash on hand in their accounts to buy stocks, bonds, mutual funds, or other securities, and will rarely borrow to buy more
- Stay with their purchases for the long haul
- Use the dollar cost averaging method to buy into the same security at regular times, regardless of price (for example, on the fifteenth and thirtieth of every month)

It's the Taxman!

Brokerage house financial advisors are trained to give advice that allows the owner of non-retirement accounts to hold the securities for as long as possible, if for no other reason than to minimize taxes. Remember, outside of a retirement account, a stock or security that is sold within one year is a short-term gain and is taxed at a higher bracket. Investors are usually more "tax conscious" and would like to avoid paying higher taxes.

OPTIONS FOR DAY TRADERS

Adjusting to the New World of Day Trading

The post-pandemic world is nothing like the one we knew before 2020. And nowhere is this more noticeable than in the financial sector, where the actions of global central banks responded to the economy's pandemic-related crash and created a new set of parameters for day traders to consider. In this section, we'll introduce and learn how to tackle these parameters.

THE POST-PANDEMIC WORLD AND ITS EFFECTS ON DAY TRADING

The COVID-19 pandemic changed the world and spurred a rebirth in day trading. At the epicenter of the seismic changes were the shutdowns and mandates for people to stay home, which led to a nearly complete standstill in the global economy. The stock market, expecting an economic depression, crashed.

As the global economy and stock markets collapsed, central banks lowered interest rates to nearly zero and flooded the financial system with newly created fiat money, also known as quantitative easing (QE). Many governments simultaneously issued checks to citizens as fiscal stimulus.

This historic infusion of money into the financial system and directly to the population led to a bottom in the stock market. With people stuck in their homes with little to do (and with their bank accounts brimming with newly minted money to spend), many people began day trading.

Meanwhile, as the world adapted to this new normal, large numbers of people began to work from home—a practice which has not been, and may never be, fully reversed. As a result, many office workers are still homebound and now work their traditional job (part-time or full-time), alternating with day trading. Others gave up their day jobs altogether and became full-time day traders.

Most importantly, the pandemic's influences on daily life and the financial markets spurred extraordinary growth in two related areas that were lesser known to the public ahead of 2020: artificial intelligence (AI) and cryptocurrencies.

THE AI EXPLOSION

The pandemic-induced stay-at-home dynamic led to behavioral changes that extended beyond day trading into home-based recreation via video gaming and streaming. Meanwhile, businesses adapted to the post-pandemic world by automating many of their operations. As a result, there was an explosive demand for new technologies: hardware to house the growing AI, and software to run it.

This new demand for technology, hardware, and automation led to a resurgence in the semiconductor and software sectors, which had been hurt badly by the falling demand fueled by the pandemic. The solution to this new technological puzzle was AI, whose influence extends beyond the physical world into the world of finance.

AI offers excellent day trading opportunities. Stocks such as NVIDIA Corp. (Nasdaq: NVDA) are day trader favorites because of their volatility. Both the intraday and day-to-day gyrations in the price of many AI-related stocks offer the opportunity to enter positions on both the long and the short side, often more than once per day.

Other highly liquid stocks, such as Alphabet Inc. (Nasdaq: GOOGL) and Microsoft (Nasdaq: MSFT), are also big players in AI and offer ample opportunities for day trading. Plus, each of these stocks can be traded via single-stock ETFs, which offer opportunities to gain from the primary trend of the stock at a lesser price. That's a great advantage for day traders with small accounts.

Finally, the AI revolution increased the use of algorithmic trading for new day traders who found it easier to trade via automation. Many of these "bot"-fueled apps are designed to trade cryptocurrencies, while some can be used to trade stocks, currencies, and other markets. Although some are free, you can also purchase subscriptions to AI-powered platforms. Two of the most popular ones are TrendSpider (https://trendspider.com) and Trade Ideas (https://trade-ideas.com). However, before investing in AI trading platforms, do your research, consider talking to other traders before signing up, and use their free trials before subscribing.

Using Single-Stock ETFs to Trade AI Stocks

Day traders can use the Direxion Daily NVDA Bull 2X Shares ETF (Nasdaq: NVDU) to trade the long side of NVDA. This ETF moves at twice the rate of shares of NVIDIA, and it trades at a much lower price than shares of the company. For example, on May 8, 2024, NVIDIA shares were trading at $905 per share, while NVDU's share price was $63.25. If you bought 100 shares of NVDU at $63.25, you would only risk $6,325. A 2% gain in NVDA would result in a 4% ($253) gain for NVDU. Compare this to buying 100 shares of NVDA, which would cost $90,500.

THE CRYPTO CONUNDRUM

Fears of a post-pandemic economic collapse boosted interest in cryptocurrencies as a refuge. Certainly, Bitcoin and Ethereum remain the largest of the group, but other cryptocurrencies are available too.

Day traders are likely best served by sticking with these two due to their liquidity. In addition, you can trade Bitcoin in fractions, known as a satoshi (after the inventor of the coin). Each satoshi is worth 0.00000001 Bitcoin. Make sure you add in commission and other costs before trading satoshis. Minimum purchases vary per platform. A general rule is to avoid purchases below $10 due to transaction costs.

You can trade cryptocurrencies directly, via an exchange, through apps, or indirectly via your futures account or through ETFs. Popular exchanges include Coinbase (www.coinbase.com) and Crypto.com (www.crypto.com). If you choose to trade through an app, you may want to consider Kraken (www.kraken.com) or Gemini (www.gemini.com).

Each individual exchange and app has its own rules, which you should review carefully before downloading and transferring money for trading. There are several examples of fraudulent activity in the crypto universe, with the Sam Bankman-Fried (also known as SBF) scandal grabbing the biggest headlines. In this case, SBF, the founder of a crypto exchange, once known as the "Crypto King," was convicted of stealing client money for personal expenses. He was found guilty and sentenced to twenty-five years.

There are also ETFs, which trade crypto futures as well as spot cryptos. Spot prices are the most current price of a coin, while futures prices are prices for a later date.

A popular Bitcoin futures ETF is the ProShares Bitcoin Strategy ETF (NYSE: BITO), which invests in Bitcoin futures. Plus, the ProShares Short Bitcoin Strategy ETF (NYSE: BITI) offers the opportunity to make money when Bitcoin futures fall. There are also leveraged ProShares Bitcoin Strategy ETFs, like the Ultra Bitcoin ETF (NYSE: BITU), which is a spot ETF that rises or falls at twice the rate of current Bitcoin prices. To play the short side, you can use the ProShares UltraShort Bitcoin ETF (NYSE: SBIT). This ETF lets you profit at twice the rate of a price decline in the spot price of Bitcoin. You can find a full listing of ProShares's crypto ETFs, including those that trade Ethereum, at www.proshares.com/fund-highlights/bito.

CryptoSlate: An Easy Source for Crypto Information

Because there are so many cryptocurrencies and there is always a great deal of activity in the sector, keeping up with daily news is paramount for day traders. A great place to find useful information is CryptoSlate (https://cryptoslate.substack .com). You can elect to pay for a subscription, but their daily free email offers a great deal of useful macro information, which may be all you need.

Chapter 2

Creating a Trading Plan

Developing a good trading plan is essential to trading success, and in many ways, it is a lot like making plans to go on vacation. You wouldn't show up at the airport without booking your tickets and knowing the flight schedule. And you certainly wouldn't fly to a distant city without preparing for your trip, or having your hotel room booked and reserved. Trading is much like that: you do best if you've planned your buys, profit points, and sell levels. You also do best knowing how to exit a trade that is going bad or, better yet, knowing when to exit a bad trade before it turns into a significant loss.

A GOOD DAY IN THE MARKETS

Viewing the News, Trading Post-Pandemic, and More

Let's take a look at what a good day for a day trader is like. Good days can be lazy or exciting, but they always come with good profits.

It's Monday morning, about 6:00 a.m. Central US time, and after you've walked the dog, you stream your new favorite show. During a slow scene, you click on your Investing.com app and see that the stock index futures are rallying. You've been expecting this since the market has been in a down draft for four days, and it is due for a bounce. You find that bond yields are back below 4% on the US Ten Year Note, the currency markets are quiet, and oil prices are stable. Plus, overnight Asian economic news sources are suggesting the Chinese economy continues to struggle while the markets are in a trading range.

SCANNING THE NEWS

The Investing.com calendar says that Monday will be a quiet day, although there is one report that may move the market: the New York Federal Reserve 1-Year Consumer Inflation Expectations. By Wednesday, things will perk up when the weekly mortgage data is released, along with the weekly oil supply numbers from the US Energy Information Administration (EIA). There are also some Federal Reserve speakers due to make remarks during the week. The big news will be the release of the US Consumer Price Index, which will be out on Thursday. You look at economic reports that are upcoming for the week and make note of the other economic and political news and how you believe it will affect the markets.

The underlying theme is inflation. You want to see how the bond and stock markets respond to the data. If the news is bullish for inflation, bonds will like it. If bonds traders see the data as favorable for inflation, they will buy bonds, yields will fall, and stocks are almost certain to rise. Because bond yields and stock index futures are constructive, you know the market has a bullish bias until proven otherwise.

THE BEGINNING OF A TRADING SETUP

While fixing breakfast, the news breaks that Saudi Arabia cut the price of oil for its customers in Asia. Oil prices fall and the bond market rallies, causing yields to fall. Oil has been falling for weeks after reaching $94 per barrel three months ago. At $75, you've made money on West Texas Intermediate (WTI) with a short e-mini oil futures trade, thinking it will go lower. (The e-mini oil is a US-based futures contract that tracks the price of WTI oil prices but is priced for a five-hundred-barrel contract value, as opposed to the full-sized contract of one thousand barrels.) *Wow*, you think, *this is going to shake up the commodities market.* The futures markets are already open in the US, and you quickly rush over to your desktop and close out your short WTI oil trade in order to catch the price drop before it bounces back. You'll watch that bounce back happen over the next few hours, allowing you to capture the gain before the temporary bounce.

Since the oil story is sure to be big news all day, you analyze what trades you could set up. Your goal is a few well-diversified intraday and perhaps overnight trades that you could close out tomorrow morning when the US traders are up and trading full blast.

GETTING YOUR TRADES PLACED

Once you've closed out the oil futures trade, you switch your trading platform to the Forex (currency trading). At 50:1 leverage, you set up a nice 10,000 USD long USD/CAD currency trade that costs you $200 of your margin account. You know this long USD/CAD trade will show a profit when the US dollar gains value against the Canadian dollar because there are rumblings in the market that the hostilities in the Red Sea stemming from the war in Gaza are causing major shipping companies to reroute their ships around the tip of Africa. This rerouting will likely lead to supply chain problems and inflationary pressures, which will cause the US Federal Reserve to keep interest rates higher for longer and possibly raise them again. Higher interest rates are bullish for the underlying currency, in this case the US dollar.

Because a higher dollar is often a negative for oil prices, you place a trade of a "2x short" leveraged oil company stock ETF on your stock brokerage trading platform. While the US markets won't be open until later this morning, you put the trade in anyway and set it for "At the Open." This means it will fire off the trade in the first seconds the market opens. You're unsure of the price, but you know it's possible that once the bounce runs its course, oil prices will continue to fall during the day—in fact, you're planning to close out this trade at the end of the trading day, after all the news stations have reported the news to US investors. Investors follow news, too, and you know they'll be calling into their brokers and selling stock in oil-producing companies throughout the day.

HEDGING YOUR TRADES

When your profit-capturing trades are set up, you call your best friend, who's also a day trader. She's watching the news too. After a laugh about all the money you guys are going to make, you discuss the best way to hedge the profit trades as cheaply and easily as possible. You both decide the best way to hedge the oil trades is by using a stock that is in a bullish trading pattern. You go through a few price charts and find that Amazon.com fits the bill; traders have been buying the shares when the price dips, and you wait for the open before pulling the trigger. The stock opens below the prior day's closing price but quickly starts to gain. That's the signal that traders who like buying on dips are moving in. You buy in at 10:00 a.m. and stick with the trade for three hours, bagging a nice $2 gain on half of the shares while keeping the other half in place.

What's a Hedge?

Traders use the word "hedge" a lot. Essentially, it's a trade you make to offset possible loss from another trade. Think of it as a kind of insurance. For example, to hedge your Amazon trade you can buy an ETF that invests in US Treasuries. Treasuries usually rally when the economy slows. This hedge would help to cushion any fall in Amazon shares if there is any news that suggests the economy is slowing and that consumers will slow down their buying.

No matter what, you put in a stop-loss order, which is designed to limit the losses in the Amazon trade. This trade will work as long as the dip buyers remain confident in their ability to buy low and sell high. By the afternoon, the stock's price is flattening out, but it's still trading above your sell stop. You decide to keep the trade open overnight and it pays off as Amazon rallies at the open the next day, and you close out the position with another $1.50 per share profit.

If it is a risk-on day for the markets around the world, the world's currencies that pay higher interest (i.e., countries with high economic growth, and higher interest rates or the potential for higher interest rates) are worthwhile risk-on trades, as they would gain in value against the currency of a country with lower economic growth. The US dollar, the euro, Japanese yen, or the Swiss franc are always worth keeping in mind. These countries are more economically established and therefore have lower growth rates than high growth economies, but are considered interest rate bellwethers. This is especially true of the dollar and the euro.

Generally, the growth economies are the developing nations such as Brazil, the currencies of southeastern Asia, and the currencies of some eastern European developing nations (such as the Czech koruna, Hungarian forint, etc.). At the same time, the currencies that are known as "commodity currencies" (i.e., from a country that produces and exports commodities as its main trade good) will also be considered a risk-on currency under the right circumstances, such as when the country's commodity production increases. This is because the economic well-being of developing nations is tied to the overall well-being of the world economy (but they are growing at a faster pace than the established countries during periods of global growth). During periods of slowing global growth, the commodity-producing economies are reliant on a strong world economy to ensure the constant demand for the goods they produce, such as oil, copper, iron ore, and so forth. The idea is: If the world's economies keep growing, there will be more and more demand for the commodities, as they will be used up in the many manufacturing processes across the globe. On the other hand, if the world's economies slow down, manufacturing will also slow, lessening demand, lowering prices, and finally causing a slowdown in the countries that produce those raw materials.

Globalization Is Shrinking

After the COVID-19 pandemic and the war in Ukraine, the global economy changed. Countries shifted to be more involved in regional trade patterns. This is likely to evolve for the foreseeable future, which means reliable trading patterns may change. This means that focusing on trading shares of companies that rely less on global sales and more on domestic markets makes sense. For example, if you've become accustomed to making money trading shares of global companies such as 3M (NYSE: MMM), expanding your horizons to US-centric companies like homebuilder D.R. Horton (NYSE: DHI) will make sense. You can also look toward companies who do most of their business in areas of the US which are growing, as opposed to those who focus on areas where populations are falling.

By doing your homework you made money in the oil, currency, and stock markets and closed out your trades with profits. Pour yourself a drink and see what develops tomorrow.

A BAD DAY IN THE MARKETS

Keeping Calm and Cool

Most of your trading days will be structured, controlled, and profitable. While your aim is always to anticipate your trades and map out your profits, some days are filled with bad news. These days can be disasters to your profits and can be nerve-wracking to go through. Here's an example of what it's like during one of the market's bad days.

YOUR OVERNIGHT TRADES ARE SET

You've had a run of good days lately, but today it's different. You've read the market and you see that there is a risk-on sentiment in the market. Basically, the rule is this: The market comes in two forms, risk-on or risk-off. You'll know it's a risk-on day when the stock market is up, your long trades are doing well, and the people on the news channels such as CNBC are excited. All is good in the market, there is nothing to worry about, and everyone seems to be getting rich. You'll know it's a risk-off day when the markets are down by large amounts (over 1%), everything on your trading screen is in "the red" (it's green when going up and red when going down in value), and when you tune into CNBC or check your favorite website for financial news and the stories are negative: All the commentators are predicting the end of good times and are openly wondering, "Is everyone losing money? Is everyone going broke?"

The market and the public are very fickle: There can be a few days of the market being risk-on, and then a few days of the market being risk-off for no apparent reason.

You've placed your risk on long AUD/CHF (Swiss francs) and long EUR/CHF trades, along with some well-thought-out automatic profit-taking stops. Going to bed, you realize that you're going to wake up with a bit of profit, feel good about the day, and go to work with a little extra money in your trading account.

THE BAD NEWS STARTS ROLLING IN

You get up, make your coffee, and begin making breakfast with CNBC on in the background. There is a lot of chatter about foreign exchange rates and an intervention of the Swiss National Bank in the market. This makes you take a pause. Turning up the volume, you realize that the Swiss National Bank has intervened in the currency market and drastically changed the exchange rate between the Swiss franc and other world currencies. The markets have reacted with turmoil overnight. Basically, the Swiss have forced the change in exchange rates after having them locked in for years. The EUR/CHF has gone from 1.10 to .98 in seconds overnight, meaning the Swiss franc has gained against the euro drastically. This has wiped out every short Swiss franc trade worldwide, yours included. Your trade was set to make money when the euro got stronger against the Swiss franc, but the opposite has happened. Now the question is, how badly has the trade affected your account?

You know bank interventions such as this are rare and can cause massive damage to an account. You look at your chart. There is a huge spike at 3:00 a.m. when the bank moved the rate. You look at the balance in your account. The FX platform has tried to hold on to your stops, but the huge number of trades worldwide that were shorting the CHF has caused the Forex broker to cause your trades to "slip" and fall before it could "stop you out" (i.e., trigger the automatic closing orders you preprogrammed to avoid losing too much on a trade). Your account slipped because of the sheer number of losing trades worldwide, and the broker's computers couldn't handle all the automatic stop-out trades firing off at the same time (when this happens, it can be a big problem!). The good thing is your trades got closed before your account totally lost out. The bad thing is, the slippage in the account caused such a delay in the stop-exit trade (the one you set up to prevent major losses) that you lost 40% of your account value within seconds. The trade closed out, but you're stuck with the deep loss on the trade.

With a racing pulse, you realize how bad this could have been for your trading account. You take some cleansing breaths, close the computer, and go through the motions of getting ready for the workday. *Good thing I have a regular job*, you think, while the newscasters on CNBC excitedly talk about the overnight currency markets. Quickly, you evaluate the rest of your positions. The long oil mini future trade is up 0.5% in early trading along with your long e-mini S&P 500 futures trade, as it is still a "risk-on day" with worldwide assets, but your e-mini gold futures is down. That's okay, because you knew that this was to be your hedge against the larger risk-on trades, and you have the overall big hedge for your monies in the Goldman Sachs Hedge Industry VIP ETF (symbol: GVIP); this is an ETF that is built to closely follow the Goldman Sachs Hedge Fund VIP Index, a widely used hedge fund value index composed of fifty stocks largely owned by hedge funds.

ASSESSING THE FINANCIAL
DAMAGE IN YOUR ACCOUNT

Overall, you realize that your account was properly hedged with the long gold futures hedge (which would go up if the markets got bad overall as a worldwide safe haven trade), and you also have the macro hedge with the hedge fund ETF. These positions have helped your account immensely: The losses haven't been that bad, as they've been properly hedged to prevent too much of a loss from one trade.

What's a Macro Hedge?

A macro hedge is a trading style that incorporates all the world's financial products and markets—gold, currencies, bonds, commodities, worldwide equities, etc.—into one balanced, internally hedged product, where you can trade one ETF to hedge your portfolio, while within that ETF there is a deeper, internal level of hedging going on: diversification within diversification.

You look further, and you realize it is still a risk-on day in the markets—you read it right—but the Swiss National Bank's interventions couldn't be predicted. While the currency account is down 40%, you've managed to hedge out enough risk so that the overall net value of your account is only down by 5%. Not too bad. After a little math, you see that you're actually okay for the day, but the whole thing has really shaken you. You know there is only one thing to do on days like this: close out all your trades and go 100% cash. Get out of the markets and cool off. It was a bad day for you and others worldwide, and there could be some massive sell-offs or risk-unwinding coming in the next few weeks, and you'd really like to sit it out. No more trading for you for a while.

Quietly, you close out all of your trades, one by one. You do this manually, with the click of a button, even though the trades look like they will be going up for the rest of the morning and you have the chance of earning more on each trade and erasing some more of your overall losses. The fact is, you and the rest of the traders worldwide are a bit shaken from the overnight news, and they are thinking the same thing: Get out now, while the getting is good, and wait for the markets to sort it out. You know markets are all linked and that the Swiss franc is heavily used to finance trading and commerce worldwide. You're thinking it could get really messy while it is sorted out, and you'd like to lessen your risk overall. By closing out your account to 100% cash, you can earn some interest while resting easy, waiting for this news to get factored into the world's markets.

WRITING A BUSINESS PLAN

Treat Day Trading Like a Business

The best way to look at day trading is to see it as a business. You will need a computer, tablet, or smartphone. You'll also need cash to fund your trading account. The good news is that you won't need a big cash outlay to start, and you can have a lot of fun with even the smallest trading account.

HOW MUCH YOU NEED TO DAY TRADE

Your investment in day trading can be as small as a few hundred dollars if you are trading in the currency markets and $1,000 if you are trading in the stock market.

Futures trading is a bit more complex—most minimum accounts are of $2,000, but due to the way the margin is settled daily, it would be best to have $2,500 or more in your account before trading. If this amount isn't in your futures account, you run the risk of getting intraday margin calls daily whenever your trading account falls below the $2,000 threshold.

What's a Margin Call?

A margin call is when the broker or exchange declares that cash must be added to your account to bring it back up to a predetermined cash balance. If you don't do this, the trades in your account will be automatically closed out. Since this can be very unprofitable, it's best to keep your futures account well above the minimum before trading.

KEEPING TRACK OF YOUR EXPENSES, GAINS, AND LOSSES

Because day trading is a business, it pays to have a budget. Keep track of your expenses such as internet, phone, and, if you have a home office, part of your mortgage or rent. You should also track the cost of subscriptions to trading magazines, newspapers, and websites. All of these expenses should appear on your profit and loss statements.

Taxes

Day trading profits are considered short-term capital gains and are therefore reported as regular income on personal tax returns. When you're successful at day trading, these gains and profit can add up quickly, amounting to hundreds or thousands of dollars a year in profits. The gains you make trading will be taxed at your regular tax rate. If you're already in a high tax bracket, the profits you make in your trading account will be taxed at this rate. This means you'll need to build in tax expenses into your trade gains along with your trading expenses ($5–$10 each into and out of your trades).

The best way to handle any kind of taxable business is to keep track of all your expenses. You can even link a debit card to the cash balance in your brokerage account. Think of it this way: You could deposit $5,000 in your stock trading account and get a debit card tied to the cash balance. A good plan would be to trade all month, booking all profits and absorbing any losses. At the end of the month your account would be higher in value than when you started. You could then take a small sum out of the account to cover the expenses associated with trading, pay those bills with the money, and leave the rest in the account to multiply and compound for the next month's trades. Your second option would be to take out the small amount to cover your expenses, along with a set "salary" or fixed cut of your trading profits. Your trading expenses would be paid, and your "salary" would go to living a better life, paying household bills, etc. You'd leave some profit in your account to build over time. While the first option makes sense in the beginning as you build up your account, the second option is the way to go if you become a full-time day trader.

TAKING YOUR PROFITS
AND TAKING A SALARY

Taking a paycheck from your trading activity makes it a job and ensures you are enjoying the profits of your day trading business.

Hoarding profits by allowing your account to grow and grow without taking out any money will defeat the purpose of day trading (to make it a career). Larger and larger trades are glamorous to be sure, but they can be difficult to manage. If the economy turns bad and if the stock market and Forex markets get rocky, you might run into difficult trading times. It's during these times that you'll be glad that you used and enjoyed some of the profits you accumulated by trading: car payments, dinners out, vacations, college tuition, etc. Good traders know to not get greedy; greed leads to poor trading decisions and risky behavior. Staying hungry with day trading can lead to safer, more profitable trading.

THE POWER OF KNOWING
YOUR PROFIT GOALS

When you're starting out, it's good to think about what you'd like to accomplish with your day trading. The best thing to do is to ask yourself what you would like to do with the money. It's good to set goals, as this will guide your trading and give you performance benchmarks, which in turn will lead to making changes as needed. If you'd like to make enough to pay for a new car payment, and you need $400 a month in extra income, then you know you'll only need to trade enough to earn this much. After your first $400 each month, you know you can stop aggressively trading since you've reached your goal. You can slow down and look for only the best trades with the least amount of risk. You can get into only the best trades and make a little more with little risk. You can also sit on the cash, patiently waiting for the next month, when you'll be at it again. This way you'll be keeping the risk profile of your account to an absolute minimum while you earn your car money.

The business plan and your goal setting can help you with your risk profile and trading frequency. You can trade as little or as much as you want, starting and ending each day with cash. If you're not meeting your goals, it's time to make changes. The key is to find the balance between profit and enjoyment of the task.

MAKING THE BEST USE OF YOUR TIME

How to Plan Your Trading Day

You can start your day by listening to the business news stations, such as CNBC or Bloomberg, while you get ready for the morning. They often offer some great insight as to what economic reports are scheduled to happen later on in the day. This serves as a good way to get into day trading early, before some of the markets open. A review of the markets can help you recognize some very profitable trading opportunities that are coming along during the day.

Useful Websites

The Investing.com app has free real-time futures, currency, commodity, and crypto quotes, along with up-to-date overnight news roundups from Asia and Europe. A great place to keep up with oil markets is OilPrice.com. And if you're a fan of real estate and housing stocks, check out TheRealDeal.com.

EARLY MORNINGS WITH THE MARKET NEWS

Reviewing the news informs you if the markets are stable or in a state of unrest. Unrest may be due to what happened overnight in the Asian or European markets, the fact that a big US economic report is coming out, or even the breakout of a war. Here's a typical scenario:

You wake up at 5:00 a.m., start the coffeemaker, read the Markets section of *The Wall Street Journal*, and glance at the morning news shows. For raw numbers, you review the stock index futures, currency pairs, and bond market prices or yields on your investing app. You note that overnight the markets in Germany and London were in disarray, and at 2:00 p.m. the US Federal Reserve will make an announcement on interest rates. Armed with this information, you could decide that it is in your best interest to take the day off from active day trading. You know you'll miss out on any upside from potential positive news made during the day. But you also know you'll insulate yourself from any whipsawing or wild swings in the markets preceding and following major news. You have to determine whether those two possible upsides are better than risking your account on a big news day.

A good solution for unpredictable market days is to trade in your practice, or demo, account—the account that your broker will give you to practice trading ideas with "play money." They might fund your account with $25,000 worth of digital play money that isn't really cash. You can log in, scout for trade setups, set stop losses, and figure out your profit points. You can even execute orders with the same live pricing that a real account would see and use, all the while using and risking only the play money in your account. Any wins or gains throughout the day would be "play wins." These accounts are handy on difficult trading days when it's best not to risk real money. They can also serve as a great testing and learning environment for you to try new trading scenarios in a real market setting.

Chapter 3

The Cost of Trading

While the profits and benefits from day trading can be considerable, there are important aspects to consider as people react differently to working on their own. You may need to balance the loneliness of working at home with planned time out of the office, for example. This is especially true within the markets, trading your money day in and day out. In most jobs, if you have a bad day, you still get paid; no money is at risk. With trading, though, you are putting money at risk, and each trade carries a possibility of loss. Your financial success or future lies almost completely in your own hands. In this chapter, we'll look at the costs of day trading—both financial and human.

WORKING ALONE

The Loneliness of Day Trading

After you determine that you can temper your emotion, know your risk tolerance, and have disposable cash to trade with, the most important question that remains is: Can you work alone? Day traders often trade in an office in their homes, away from the business and financial districts of their hometowns or nearby cities. Doing this, you may miss the interaction with coworkers, the friendly chats with other commuters on the train going to work, or even the act of walking down to the corner coffee shop with an office friend for a much-needed afternoon break.

Working alone means no access to coworkers to speak with about things such as last night's game, or to discuss your trading ideas. You might even find yourself wishing that you could approach a manager or boss about a trade you are about to make involving more than the usual amount of your money. In these cases, you might find it comforting to have a superior to help shoulder the burden of your decisions. However, that's not part of day trading. All the cash, knowledge, skill, and risk-taking are yours and only yours. So, though day trading alone has multiple benefits, you should consider if the business is right for your temperament. Here are some positive and negative aspects to consider when working alone as a day trader:

Working Alone As a Day Trader
- There is no one checking your attendance.
- There is no one to make sure you are at your desk for the opening bell.
- There is no accounting department to record your gains and losses.

- There is no technical department to fix your software/computer.
- There is no one to delegate tasks to, such as printing, faxing, filing, or running out for sandwiches.
- There is no such thing as a paid sick day.
- There is no need for nice clothes to wear to the office.

Like most day traders, you will probably decide that working alone has its upsides. In fact, the list of benefits that come from successfully day trading well outnumbers the negatives. Most of the challenges associated with day trading revolve around the psychology of being responsible for gains and losses, and to your ownership of your trades and trading account. Because you are the only one who makes the decisions about your day trading career and your account, the only performance review that matters will be the satisfaction that you are building up your account (and net worth) through your day trading efforts over time.

It's a Business, so Treat It Like One

- Show up for work at regularly scheduled times.
- Set up your office to allow for natural light and, if possible, views of outside.
- Dress for success. Wear your "work clothes" if this gives you a more professional attitude, as this might make you feel like you are on the clock.
- Keep accurate records of your trading decisions and give yourself periodic reviews of your trading activity, accounting for your decisions that led to successes and failures.
- Schedule vacations with family or friends at regular times throughout the year, just like you do with a normal job.
- Create a routine, both for starting and ending your day.

- Stay in touch with people; just walking to the neighborhood coffee shop or driving to the market can offer refreshing opportunities for contact with others.

Keeping a Clear Head and Staying in the Game for the Long Haul

Starting the trading day with exercise gives you the energy required for a long vigil in front of the trading screen. A good brisk early morning walk with your dog or loved one starts things off in the right direction. On cold days it helps to have an exercise bike in the house. But the best way to stay in the game is to know when to shut things down. If you've had a profitable day, there is no reason to look for overnight trades. Take the night off; enjoy dinner at your favorite restaurant or have a cozy night with takeout and a good show on your favorite streaming site. Day trading is a job, which when managed correctly will offer many rewards. But it's not a sprint; it's a marathon.

THE DAY TRADER'S TOOLS

Trade Like a Pro

Look at trading as a job and your trading account as your tools. A mechanic would be excited when a customer brought in a Ferrari to be worked on, but he would perform the tune-up with a cool professionalism that is separate from his love of Italian cars. He would not abuse his wrenches or gauges in such a way as to diminish their value or harm them—or the car—in any way. This is a good way to think about trading and your trading account. You will be working on very expensive, exotic things while using your precious tools of the trade—i.e., you will trade a particular sector using your precious trading account.

KEEP A COOL HEAD

This idea of trading as a professional and treating trading like a business is one of the key elements to a successful long-term day trading career. Your emotions will be tied to every trade before it is made, but you don't have to let them overwhelm you. You can learn to use a cool head to plan entry points (the point at which you make your initial purchase of a stock, commodity, or currency), as well as using calm, calculated strategies to exit trades and capture profits. There are many stories of day traders feeling elated with their unrealized gains on a trade (unrealized means the profits are still "on paper" and not yet in the day trader's account, as the trade has not been closed out yet) and not being emotionally able to exit the trade in hopes of yet more gains.

Trades Gone Bad

In day trading, good management of your emotions is equated to sound money management. When things go wrong, day traders second-guess their actions, often saying they "should have taken the profits," and asking, "what was I thinking?" If you manage your emotions, you can make money on good trading days and keep more of your money on bad trading days. So, set limits on profits and losses. Once you hit your target profit, it's time to sell—there are always other trades.

TIME COMMITMENT

The second thing to consider before you begin your day trading career is how to make the time commitment. Depending on how much you already know about markets, it can take anywhere from one month to several seasons to get enough general knowledge to begin successfully trading. At the minimum, you must commit to a structured study period for a few weeks to get acquainted with the markets. Read books and check out online business newspapers designed for independent day traders, such as *The Wall Street Journal*, or other news websites and channels such as Investing.com, *Investor's Business Daily*, Bloomberg, and CNBC.

Too often, people want to start placing trades and making profits immediately. However, to maximize your chances of success, it's best to take your time to learn how the markets work before committing any money. There are stories of people opening an account online in a matter of minutes, depositing money, and rushing to trade. There are also stories of day traders placing trades in fresh accounts when they aren't even sure how to use the trade input screens. They make trades in the wrong direction, for the wrong amounts, and often lose all their money in a hurry. You can avoid these failures by taking your time while opening an account, learning how to operate it, and learning what you would like to trade through practice trades.

Once you are in full swing, you'll find time speeding by as you sit in front of your computer, trying to capture the gains of the market as it moves up and down. While some markets can be traded into the evening and overnight, most of them are open only during the mornings and early afternoons. This means that to day trade, you must be available to follow news, read charts, and place trades during these hours. It is also possible to trade part time. Some trades can be made on Sunday afternoons and after work during the week. If you would like to begin your day trading on a part-time basis, then this is a good option for you. Just allow yourself enough time to learn the market on your shortened schedule.

AVAILABLE CASH

All jobs require tools and equipment. If you are a plumber, you might need a van to haul your plumbing equipment. A painter needs brushes and ladders. Accountants can't function without computers and tax software. When you are a day trader, your equipment is your trading account. It's usually filled with a combination of cash and margin. Just as a plumber needs a certain size van, you will need a certain amount of money to begin day trading.

When you're just starting out, you can do well with a small amount of cash. You can have a lot of fun and learn a lot with as little as $250 in your account. For example, if you have $250 in your foreign exchange trading account, you could spend the night making small, quick trades while watching television. It is possible to do this each night and make enough money to pay for your breakfast doughnut, lunch, and afternoon coffee all on the profits you make from the night before. This can actually be a really good way to get used to the market lingo, software, and the process of order entry all while building a positive trading experience.

TRADING WITH SMALLER ACCOUNTS

Don't worry if you have a small amount of money in your account. This is normal when your start. Certainly, trading with small amounts can be quite fulfilling, but it can tempt you into foolish mistakes. You may argue that because you have a smaller dollar amount in your trading account, you should make high-risk/reward trades. After all, even if they go wrong, you won't lose that much money. Resist this thinking. If you do this with a small account, you'll keep the bad habits, which will make your problems worse if you move to a larger account. Improper position size, margin mismanagement, and a series of misplaced trades can lead to losses that can close out any account, regardless of its size.

If you start small and get used to the feeling of winning a trade you planned, you're programming your brain for success. As time passes, you can gradually add to your account and trade larger and larger amounts. You will, however, need to have enough discretionary money from your normal household budget to use for trading. It's not a good idea to trade with your rent or car payment money. Only trade with money that is earmarked for your trading account—i.e., it should be money that you are able to lose or at least use for a risky venture such as day trading. After you are up and running as a full-time professional day trader, you will be able to make periodic withdrawals from your account as a salary draw. Until then, the money you use to trade should be allowed to grow with each winning trade.

BROKERAGE BASICS

Choosing a Brokerage Firm

Before you begin your day trading career, you will have to choose a brokerage firm. Think of this selection process much like an interview for a job vacancy you have at your day trading firm. First, there are the basic interview questions to ask: Can the broker do the job? Does he have the skills to succeed? These questions are worth keeping in mind. And second, you need to know if the candidate is a good "fit" with your day trading company.

TYPES OF FIRMS

When choosing a brokerage firm you will have different options, depending upon the type of sector you are interested in and your opening balance.

BROKERAGE FIRMS		
TYPE	BENEFIT	DISADVANTAGE
Deep-discount online firms	Good for stocks and ETFs	Not broker assisted
FX brokerage firms	Low account minimums, high margin	Not broker assisted
Multisector firms	Low-to-mid account minimums, high margin	Not broker assisted
Combination firms	Broker assistance, multiple sectors	High minimums
Full-service firms	Excellent source of trading information, broker assistance for setting up complex trades, multiple sectors	High minimums, high transaction costs

Discount Firms

The first type of brokerage firm you can consider is the deep-discount firm, which only offers services online. These brokerages will offer a discount on the price if you exceed a certain number of trades, usually fifty in a month. If you plan to do Forex trading, be ready for a completely hands-off approach from the brokerage firm. Many do not offer any broker assistance and often offer only limited technical assistance, if any at all.

FX Brokerage Accounts

If you plan to day trade in an FX account, you will need to keep good records of your cash deposits, cash withdrawals, and all the gains and losses for each trading day. These firms will not send you a statement every month and will not list the trades you make over the quarter or year. Most likely they will keep track of your overall profit and loss as it accumulates in your account, but often this will roll over from year to year. Considering this, with the FX accounts and others that do not send you a statement (or send you a loosely based one), it is best to keep track of your profits, losses, and interest earned on a daily profit and loss sheet.

You Get What You Pay For

As a general rule, the more services provided by a Forex broker will increase your required minimum account balances. This type of account, which often requires minimum balances of $5,000–$10,000, offers more services and is called a standard account. A bare bones account, which lets you trade with small amounts of money—sometimes as low as a $250 minimum—is often called a mini account.

Foreign currency brokers usually charge low commissions on popular pairs, called majors. Higher commissions are charged on other currency pairs, or crosses, consisting of two major currencies that are less commonly paired. The highest commissions are charged on infrequently traded pairs, referred to as exotics. These are any of the pairs that involve the developing countries (even if the other currency is a major FX such as the EUR or USD). Examples of this include the US dollar/Brazil real (USD/BRL), the euro/Czech koruna (EUR/CZK), and the euro/Hungarian forint (EUR/HUF). The pairs may also include some of the developing nations of Asia. The more infrequently an exotic is traded, the more expensive it can become. On the other hand, the cheapest FX pair to trade is always the EUR/USD, as this is the most heavily traded currency pair in the world. Since the costs of the commissions and brokerage fees are subtracted from your overall profit, it makes sense to try to get the lowest fees possible for each round trip of trading. Some commissions are a flat rate, with larger amounts, and effectively will put you at a loss even before you start to trade.

FX Pricing and Pips

FX brokerage accounts set their pricing in a different way than a typical stock brokerage account. They usually have a set percentage of the currency amount of the currency pairs posted in their commission structure. The commission is deducted automatically from your trade balance after the trade is placed. This has the net effect of putting you at a loss at the moment of the trade. The commission is based upon hundredths of a percent, often referred to as basis points. These basis points commissions are called pips—i.e., each basis point is a pip. The pip price that you pay for your trade will stay the same regardless of the size of the trade. In other words, if the commission structure for a EUR/USD trade is 1 pip and you place a trade of 10,000 EUR/USD, the commission will be 1 EUR for the round trip of the trade. If you place a trade for $1 million EUR/USD, the commission will be 100 EUR for one complete opening and closing of the trade. The charge will be taken out at the time of the trade; on the other hand, if you traded stocks or ETFs, you would be charged for buying and then again when you sell. Each time you buy and sell is a separate cost.

Multisector Brokerage Firms

The lack of records provided by a brokerage firm should not prevent you from considering whether it fits your needs in other matters. Perhaps you would like to trade gold, oil, and FX; in that case, you would do well by opening up a multisector account. Multisector brokerage accounts usually have a higher minimum than the pure FX accounts, as the lot size or smallest trade size in the other sectors might require a higher minimum account cash balance to trade effectively. For example, some brokerage firms offer full multisector accounts with 200:1 margin with an opening deposit of $2,500. Again, with this type of account you would not get any type of broker assistance in setting up trades, and you would not get any type of statement from the firm. You can keep track of your daily net gains, losses, and interest earned using preprinted paper trading forms. These forms also have places to record the stock index levels and overall market conditions present during that day. They can be used for tax purposes and to have a permanent record of your trading successes.

Combination Brokerage Firms

Combination brokerage firms have licensed brokers available to assist in setting up trades and hedge trades. They have two types of pricing structures: one for online trading at the discount rate, and one for broker-assisted trades at a higher, full-service rate. This higher rate can be worth the price if you are just starting out, setting up a complicated trade, or would just like to "talk through" the logic of a trade before making a commitment to it.

Full-Service Brokerage Accounts

Going through a full-service brokerage firm will help greatly if you're planning to invest, even though the high commissions will prevent you from day trading in this type of account. The research and education supplements provided by full-service firms are useful in your day trading career. However, you can get excellent information, often free of charge, online. While full-service brokers offer overall market analysis, sector and industry-specific analysis, and information regarding the trading potential of the S&P 500, ETFs, commodities, and currencies, your goal should be to become your own market analyst and self-directed trader.

If you choose to get access to Wall Street research and day trading ideas, even if you have to pay for it, you can get in through the back door by opening an account at a full-service brokerage firm that offers insight into the markets you are trading in. You can do this by putting your "other" money into this account—i.e., roll over your 401(k), open an IRA, or set up a retail brokerage account with your investments, long-term money, or mortgage. In this case you would use the full-service brokerage firm for your long-term investment (not day trading) money. You could then have access to their brokerage reports, research, and daily market, Forex, and commodities reports. You could have an account at one of these firms and subscribe to their email list for their daily reports. These reports are usually well written and geared toward the institutional investor, offering daily in-depth analyses and recommendations, providing an essential tool for the active day trader.

The yearly price the full-service brokerage firms charge to keep the account open can be anywhere from $75–$250, but the benefits of having access to all their reports and information are worth the price.

STANDARD ACCOUNTS

Standard accounts usually only allow you to trade stocks and ETFs. These accounts do not allow trading on margin, meaning you will only have the buying power of your cash balance. Standard accounts are good for beginners, because the lack of a margin limits position size and risk. Additionally, you will be limited to long-only trades, a trade in which the stock or ETF gains in value when its price goes up.

FUNDING YOUR BROKERAGE ACCOUNT

Some brokers require account liquidations to be the exact method of account funding. In other words, if you put money into your account by check, wire, credit card, or PayPal, it will have to be liquidated in the same way. The money will have to come in and out using the same method. This is important when you are planning to make biweekly or monthly withdrawals from your account as a salary draw.

Your bank may charge a fee for sending funds to your account via federal wire; check with them about this. Fees for outgoing wires can range anywhere from $35–$75 per wire. Outgoing wires are usually only processed at the beginning of the day, Monday through Friday. This account funding method will work especially well if you are sending larger amounts, as the fees associated with the wire are fixed regardless of the fund amount, acting as a volume discount. With a bank-to-bank "Fedwire" (money that is sent from account to account through the Federal Reserve's automated clearinghouse system [ACH]), a deposit is considered "good funds," meaning you can trade with them at the moment of the deposit without waiting for them.

The slowest method of all is to send a check or to walk into a freestanding brokerage office. This may be a nice day trip, especially since there are usually people sitting in the lobby and there's free coffee with CNBC or Bloomberg playing on the television. These traditional methods cost only the price of a postage stamp or a trip to the gas (or charging) station and can be a happy medium between the cost associated with wires and alternative funding methods such as PayPal and debit cards. You will have to plan when and how much you will be sending, as it will take until the check arrives (or until it can be processed after your in-person deposit) and clears before you can trade with those funds.

Chapter 4

Getting Started in the Marketplace

You've learned a bit about the markets, trading, and day trading. Next, you'll need to learn the best place to start: what to trade, how to look for trades with profit potential, and ways to get as much experience as possible entering and exiting trades.

With so many choices, it's understandable to feel nervous. A simple solution is to trade what you know or what you're most comfortable with. If you're not sure, then using your paper trading account will help you decide. Try trading different asset classes on paper for a few days each and settle on the one with which you are most comfortable.

TRADING STOCKS

A Great Place to Start

Before you begin to day trade, you must determine what you would like to trade. There are several areas of the markets to choose from. The first one we'll consider is stocks. This is a great place to start because it is easy to understand what you'll be trading.

STOCKS: PIECES OF A COMPANY

Stocks are pieces of public companies. Each share reflects a portion of the market's perceived value of the overall company. Shareholders are part owners of the company. A share of XYZ Company is the legal equivalent of part ownership of every desk, truck, building, and piece of property on XYZ's balance sheet, as well as the company's cash and future earnings.

Caps

Stocks are divided into groups depending upon their market cap (short for capitalization). The market cap is the number of shares outstanding in the market multiplied by the price of the share. For example, if XYZ Company has one million shares outstanding and each share of XYZ stock is $10, the market cap of XYZ is $10 million or 1,000,000 × $10.

If a trader thinks a stock is cheap, she will buy it, and if a different trader thinks of the stock as expensive, he will sell it. A stock's price will move up and down as it is bought and sold, as if it is caught in a constant tug-of-war. This action creates an opportunity for you as the day trader to ride the movements up and down, piggyback-style, capturing profits as you move in and out of the trades.

Interest Rates and Stock Trends

The most important influence on the general price trend for stocks is interest rates. Lower interest rates usually lead to higher stock prices. Higher interest rates usually lead to the opposite.

Central banks, such as the US Federal Reserve, raise and lower interest rates in response to inflation and economic activity. Low inflation and low economic growth lead central banks to lower their interest rates.

When central banks raise or lower interest rates, treasury bond yields usually follow their lead. Sometimes, treasury bond yields rise or fall in anticipation of a move by the central bank. Trends in yields for treasury bonds can be as strong an influence on stock prices as moves by central banks.

The Pros and Cons of Day Trading Stocks

One of the benefits of day trading stocks is that they are easy to research. Almost all brokerages offering day trading capabilities allow access to high-quality, in-house research that you can cross-check with the research put out by independent firms. Trading individual stocks also offers the opportunity for large percentage movements (2%–5% or more per day) when a stock is in play. A stock (or other investment) is in play when some news has come out that concerns the company and the news has caused other traders to take notice, making the price rise or fall.

An example is when a large retail chain reports earnings; let's say the analysts and traders have anticipated the company did really well the previous quarter (such as during the holiday season) but when the chain makes the official profit announcements, it is only half of what everyone expected. This is terrible news for the stock, which in market jargon is known as "missing the estimates" and the stock's price tumbles like a rock falling into a ravine. Not only is this news terrible for that stock, but all other retailers in the same or similar market sector that sold the same type of product are now under huge selling pressure, as the traders expect similar profit and sales figures from all similar retail stores. This is very common and results from other traders taking notice of the miss. On the other hand, if the company announces better-than-expected results, it's known as a "beat." When stocks "beat" expectations, they usually rise in price and the good news often spreads throughout the entire sector of the market.

A downside of day trading individual stocks is the tendency of traders to develop a trading portfolio of undiversified positions, which leads to a concentration of risk. Think of the "don't put too many of your eggs in one basket" adage. Sometimes being undiversified works, and sometimes it doesn't. At other times, a stock in your trading portfolio can be "stuck in the mud" and falls out of other traders' sights, leading to stagnant trading days. Your money could be tied up in a stock that doesn't move enough to make a profitable trade. This puts that amount of your tradable cash or margin at risk.

Another drawback of day trading stocks is that your margin is greatly limited compared to FX or futures. Think of margin as a revolving credit card with which to day trade. There are regulations as to the amount of margin (or credit) you can use for different sectors. Some sectors, such as stocks, are limited to around 50% of your total account including all stock and cash positions.

EXCHANGE-TRADED FUNDS

We discussed exchange-traded funds (ETFs) a bit earlier, but now we're going to talk about them in more detail. ETFs are "baskets" of individual stocks or other underlying products. They are subject to the same valuation procedures as individual stocks, but they offer the diversification function of a mutual fund—many stocks under one roof. The mutual-fund-like property of ETFs can be a real advantage, as the diversified basket reduces the concentration risk of individual stocks. At the same time, when you day trade ETFs you can capture the price movements of an entire industry sector such as financial company stocks, oil company stocks, or technology/biotechnology stocks. Certain sectors are in play at different times and are influenced by different factors. Thus, day trading ETFs can offer a very neat, compact, and effective way to trade a whole sector when that sector is moving rapidly and is in play.

Flexibility in Trading ETFs

You can use an ETF to day trade almost any type of position. There are even ETFs that offer a "short" position, allowing you to make money when the group of stocks targeted by the ETF's design goes down in value. These ETFs are often called bear funds.

The Pros and Cons of Day Trading ETFs

On the positive side, day trading ETFs offers built-in diversification, multisector availability, and their popularity with traders and institutional investors, which makes them liquid assets. Liquidity refs to the availability of money in an asset class. The more liquid the asset, the better it is as a trading vehicle. Liquidity translates to relative safety and offers improved day trading opportunities. The downside to day trading ETFs is that your trading margin will be restricted to the same amount as individual stocks, as ETFs are traded on the same exchanges as most individual stocks and are regulated as such.

DAY TRADING FOREIGN EXCHANGE

Dealing in Cryptocurrency, Gold, and More!

After you gain experience in the relatively simple world of individual stocks and ETFs, you may want to enter the world of day trading foreign exchange, gold, commodities, and futures. These sectors can allow a day trader to amplify each trade, as the allowable margin ratios can be quite large.

WHAT SETS FOREIGN EXCHANGE APART

Day trading in the foreign exchange (FX) market has become one of the preferred areas for traders looking to make a living by trading. It is an unregulated market, open around the world, trading twenty-four hours a day from Sunday afternoon to Friday afternoon.

Trading FX differs from other types of trading in a variety of ways. The first difference is what is being traded. As opposed to companies, baskets of companies, or a commodity, what you are trading is the difference between the exchange rates of two currencies. For example, you could place trades on the supposition that the Australian dollar will strengthen against the Japanese yen (AUD/JPY), the US dollar will strengthen against the Swiss franc (USD/CHF), or the Norwegian krone will get stronger against the euro (NOK/EUR).

You sell, or short, the currency you think will go down and use the money to buy, or long, the currency you think will go up.

ADVANTAGES TO DAY TRADING FX

One benefit of day trading FX is the low minimum account openings. Some brokerages allow you to open with $25 and some as low as $1. How can trades with such low amounts be made effectively? It's because FX margin ratios can be anywhere from 10:1 to as much as 500:1 in some European- and Asian-based Forex brokers. That means you could trade $50,000 worth of currency with only $100 in your account. This leverage offers the potential to make large sums of money with small amounts.

There are only about fifteen currencies that have enough volume for FX brokers to offer for trading (EUR/USD, AUD/JPY, CAD/USD, etc.), while there is a lot less to study and learn, so you can quickly get a feel for the market. Trends in the FX market are easy to recognize, which offers easy-to-find trading ideas. In addition, FX lends itself well to both economic and news analysis as well as technical chart trends. Traders look to the economic reports published by the major world central banks to value the currency pairs. Also, the study of technical charts can easily show when a currency pair is stretched (has gone too far in one direction) and is due for a correction.

Some currency pairs such as AUD/JPY are linked to stock traders' risk appetite and thus move in tandem with the world's stock markets. When traders want to accept more risk into their portfolios and buy more stock, the risky Australian dollar will also appreciate against the lower risk, traditionally safer Japanese yen.

Individual currencies are often referred to as "high yielding" and "low yielding." This refers to the general status of interest rates in each country relative to other countries. Traditionally speaking, currencies from countries such as Australia, where interest rates are higher in relative terms to other countries, such as Japan, are referred to as "high yielding."

Central Bank Intervention

Central banks are very aware of when their country's currency becomes over- or undervalued in relation to their main trading partners. When this happens, central banks intervene in the currency markets to force the adjustment of their currency. In these instances, central banks buy or sell their currency in the open market. When they buy the currency, they are looking to increase its value. When they sell their currency, they are looking to decrease its value. Interventions can create a wonderful day trading opportunity, because a whole country's financial reserves are working to move the markets.

THE DIFFICULTIES OF FX DAY TRADING

On the downside, trends in FX can develop quickly and unpredictably. FX markets are influenced by external developments, such as economic and geopolitical news including unemployment figures, military skirmishes, and other unexpected events like natural disasters. Other news and events influencing the FX market are sudden (or not so sudden) central bank interest rate changes. For example, a Pacific Rim central bank, such as the Reserve Bank of Australia, may increase its interest rates overnight while you sleep, causing a long-lasting "jump" in the value of the Australian dollar (AUD) against a lower-yielding currency such as the Swiss franc (CHF). This could cause serious problems with any short AUD/CHF positions you might have been holding overnight with thoughts that the safe-haven Swiss franc would appreciate against the high-yielding Australian dollar.

The Downside of Margin in FX

The large amounts of margin in FX can work for or against you. This depends on whether you're on the right or wrong side of a trade. Once you get used to the amount of leverage in your FX account and learn how to use it safely, it can be a very effective tool to amplify your profits. If used excessively, however, it can lead to large losses quickly.

CRYPTOCURRENCIES

Cryptocurrencies, such as Bitcoin (BTC) and Ethereum (ETH), burst onto the scene in the early 2010s and are a trillion-plus-dollar market. Unlike treasury bonds, commodities, and stocks, there are few tangible relationships tethered to their prices. Thus, day trading them is best done via technical means based on price chart analysis.

As time passes, reliable relationships to economic data are likely to develop. Moreover, the availability of "crypto" ETFs, featuring futures and spot prices, will also increase their popularity and usefulness for day traders. There may be days when stocks, bonds, and Forex don't offer opportunities to day trade. On those days, it's good to have crypto as an alternative.

GOLD AS A CURRENCY

If you are thinking that the FX market might be a good place to trade, you might also consider the gold market. Day trading gold is unique, because you have to think of it as both a commodity and a currency.

Why is gold a currency? This is because the price of gold often moves in the opposite direction of the value of paper money such as the US dollar, the British pound, and the euro. While there is a relatively fixed amount of gold, there is an ever-changing amount of printed and electronic money available. When there is more money in circulation, the price of gold goes up because there is more money bidding on the same amount of gold.

Study the potential for gold trading beginning in the early fall to get a feel for where the gold market will be heading—usually up! This is because physical gold is heavily purchased and given as gifts during the Indian marriage season in the fall and the Chinese New Year in the spring.

Gold, Inflation, and Central Bank Price Distortion

Gold is traditionally seen as a valuable measure on inflation. The traditional view is that the more the market thinks there is potential for inflation, the more traders will bid up the price of gold. The opposite traditionally holds true: the rosier and more positive the economic picture, the more traders will sell gold, causing the price to go down. However, this is true to a lesser degree in the present as central banks buy and sell gold strategically in order to maintain the value and stability of paper currencies and to reduce the market's reliance on gold as an inflation indicator.

The Benefits of Day Trading Gold

Before central banks perfected the art of buying and selling gold to maintain the value of their currencies, trading gold was simpler than other trading markets. On paper, you can argue that it's easier to read the fundamentals of a potential trade when there are relatively few influencing factors. For example, a 400-ounce brick of gold (the size of the gold bars that are stored in the vaults at Fort Knox) will never go bankrupt. Unlike corporations, gold has no balance sheet, no debt, and no product to sell. Also, there is a limited amount of gold, and it will most likely be in demand for some time.

The Problems with Day Trading Gold

Aside from central bank price manipulation, gold prices are subject to geopolitical as well as economic news, both of which can be fast coming and unannounced (with often illogical effects on the market). Because of the limited amount of gold available to trade, both central banks and major institutional investors (such as hedge funds) can have a big influence on the price of gold in the market. Lastly, the nature of gold's day tradable products, mainly ETFs and futures, offer downsides themselves: low available margin for ETFs and high minimum account size for futures.

COMMODITIES

Raw Materials

Commodities are also known as raw materials or hard assets. They are a day trader's dream when there is a strong economy. Yes, they lost some of their steam after the banking crisis took hold in late 2008, but after the pandemic, due to supply chain distortions and geopolitical issues, they once again picked up steam. Because commodities are very sensitive to supply and demand, those that are out of favor can suddenly become market leaders; thus they remain many traders' favorite vehicles.

EASY-TO-UNDERSTAND MOVEMENTS

Unlike cryptocurrencies, commodities offer easy-to-understand reasons for price movement. Their prices are tied to the world's economies and their interactions with geopolitical developments, weather, and other factors that influence the flow of supply and demand. When the economies of the world are doing well, or when there are scarcities, the prices of commodities usually go up. This upward trend can play out over days, seasons, and years. When commodities are in play, the price trends can last for extended periods. Following is a table of commodities, including the size of the smallest contract available, the exchange they are listed on, and the hours they are traded.

TYPES OF TRADABLE COMMODITIES			
COMMODITY	CONTRACT SIZE	EXCHANGE	TRADING HOURS
Corn	5,000 bushels	CBOT	Sunday–Friday 7–7:45 p.m. and Monday–Friday 8:30 a.m.–1:20 p.m. Central
Oats	5,000 bushels	CBOT	Sunday–Friday 7–7:45 p.m. and Monday–Friday 8:30 a.m.–1:20 p.m. Central
Soybeans	5,000 bushels	CBOT	Sunday–Friday 8 p.m.–8:45 a.m. and Monday–Friday 9:30 a.m.–2:20 p.m. Eastern
Copper	25,000 pounds	COMEX	6:00 p.m. Sundays–5:15 p.m. Fridays Eastern (there is a sixty-minute break each day beginning at 5:00 p.m.)
Platinum	50 troy ounces	NYMEX	8:20 a.m.–2:30 p.m. Eastern
Silver	5,000 troy ounces	COMEX	6:00 p.m. Sundays–5:15 p.m. Fridays Eastern (there is a sixty-minute break each day beginning at 5:00 p.m.)
Light sweet crude oil	1,000 barrels	NYMEX	6:00 p.m. Sundays–5:00 p.m. Fridays Eastern (there is a sixty-minute break each day beginning at 5:00 p.m.)
Heating oil no. 2	42,000 gallons	NYMEX	6:00 p.m. Sundays–5:00 p.m. Fridays Eastern (there is a sixty-minute break each day beginning at 5:00 p.m.)
Gasoline—NY unleaded	42,000 gallons	NYMEX	6:00 p.m. Sundays–5:00 p.m. Fridays Eastern (there is a sixty-minute break each day beginning at 5:00 p.m.)
Natural gas	10,000 million BTUs	NYMEX	9:00 a.m.–2:30 p.m. Eastern

COMMODITIES AND THE
WORLD'S ECONOMIES

Commodities can be an inflation trade, like gold, but they are more individually tied to their own status of supply and demand. Inflation is a sign of both scarcity and excessive amounts of money chasing tight supplies of goods. Thus, commodity prices can rise when the world is in high production mode combined with supply constraints. This can happen during periods where building, expanding, and manufacturing are growing, and during times of tight supplies for extraordinary reasons. For example, when the world emerged from the pandemic, there was an increase in demand for houses outside of cities. This spurred a building boom during periods of tight supplies for building materials right after the Federal Reserve increased the money supply via quantitative easing (aggressive money printing).

Under normal times, commodity prices rise because the goods and raw materials are the building blocks of manufactured goods (i.e., more steel is needed to manufacture more cars, more concrete for buildings and roads, etc.). Rapidly expanding countries such as China and India have a huge demand for raw materials when their economies are moving ahead strongly. With this in mind, commodities can have a unidirectional trend in good times. This means that while the price of oil and copper go up and down on a daily basis, the net trend over an economic period can generally be up for several years. Thinking in net long (over time, an average of more long positions than short positions) takes guesswork out of trading, and you will capture the slowly creeping trend to more and more expensive hard assets.

No matter the economic background, commodities are not the source of inflation, but a sign of inflationary conditions. Commodity bull markets flourish when there is tight supply, high demand, and lots of money is available in the system to drive prices higher. Commodity bear markets result when these conditions are reversed.

HARD ASSETS CAN BE UNCORRELATED TO THE STOCK MARKET

Hard asset prices (non-paper assets) are not necessarily related to the general trend in the stock market. Thus, commodities such as oil, corn, and copper can rise and fall independently of the stock market's changes. That's why knowing how to trade commodities offers an alternative market to trade when the global stock markets are moving sideways, aka consolidating.

The Subtleties of Commodity Prices

Commodities often trade based on seasonal influences. Gasoline usually gets expensive during the summer driving months, and natural gas and heating oil often rise in the winter months. Day trading commodities such as grains and petroleum can produce profits related to unpredictable extreme weather, natural and man-made disasters, and geopolitical concerns. For example, heavy rains or drought in the Midwest can affect the price of live cattle, hogs, and grains, while orange juice usually goes up in price after an unusual cold snap in Florida. Seasonal trends, however, can be affected by the status of supply and demand during the season.

Rapid, sudden movements in prices are a day trader's opportunity to make profits. When a commodity, ETF, or other tradable vehicle is in play, it is always possible to make money quickly. One trading day in May 2010, the stock market made a 9% plunge in a matter of hours. It recovered most of its losses by the end of the day, and the next Monday the S&P went up another 4%! If you entered the market at the bottom and got out of the market by the end of the day, you had a very profitable trading experience indeed.

MORE ABOUT COMMODITIES

Although there are commodities ETFs available to trade, most day trading in commodities is done in the futures markets. Trading commodities futures requires large account minimums, large amounts of leverage, and early-to-midday trading hours. If you are starting with a small amount of money or are building up your skills while keeping your full-time job, perhaps you should consider commodities after you have made the transition to day trading as your full-time career.

FUTURES

The Ultimate Paper Asset

When people say they trade futures, they mean they are trading fixed-sized contracts that allow the holder to buy or sell an underlying product at a set price at a named date in the future. Futures specify the number of units per contract and a settlement date, both of which are set by the exchanges and can't be modified. This means that each contract for each type of commodity or stock future is identical in its contents to other contracts of the same type. Additionally, there are full-sized and mini contracts: for example, a full-sized WTI oil contract is always for 1,000 barrels of oil, and a mini WTI oil contract is always for 500 barrels of oil. The same goes for wheat, corn, gold, silver, etc. contracts.

All like contracts are uniformly interchangeable. Each futures contract has a buyer and a seller. One of the parties involved in the trade is a hedger and one is a speculator. The hedger enters into the contract to offset the risk that the future price of the product will move up or down against her price. The speculator is the pure trader, who has no need to enter into a trade to hedge his corn crop, fuel for his fleet of airplanes, etc. The speculator only trades for financial gain. The hedger or the speculator can be a buyer or seller: it is the nature of the purpose of the trade that determines if it is a hedge.

An Example of a Futures Trade

An airline expects the price of jet fuel to rise substantially in the next six months. This price increase could cut into the company's profit. To hedge the risk, the company buys an oil futures contract with a set price for oil six months in the future in an effort to lock in the price of jet fuel for the fleet. The company locks in a price that it can afford to pay for fuel and still make an acceptable profit from normal flying operations. With the contract, the company is hedging the expected fuel expense, risk-managing the future expenses and profit of the company.

The other side of the trade is the purchase of the contract by a speculator, who does not have an actual need for oil or jet fuel. Instead, the speculator is betting that the price of oil will be less in the next six months than the contract price and sells the futures contract to the airline. The speculator makes money on the long side via a futures contract when the locked-in price of the contract is less than the actual price of the commodity. For example, if you buy one crude oil contract in July for oil to be delivered in November at $75 a barrel, and the actual price of crude oil moves above the $75 contract price, the value of your futures contract will move in tandem to these price movements. If oil moves to $90 by the time the contract expires, you own one thousand barrels of oil that cost you $75 per barrel, which you can then turn around and sell for $90 per barrel. Your profit will be $15 × 1,000 barrels, or $15,000. These contracts are bought and sold in huge quantities daily, creating a very liquid and profitable market for day trading.

A RANGE OF PRODUCTS

You can trade futures contracts ranging from commodities to financial products such as T-bill and US Treasury bond futures, foreign exchange futures, and S&P 500 futures. With their set contract size and delivery dates, these contracts can be traded year-round worldwide. The futures market is deep (well-financed and liquid) and international, with many institutional traders and companies coming together. A Swiss food company might enter into a US dollar futures trade and offset it with the purchase of a wheat future. With this they can lock in the exchange rate from Swiss francs to US dollars and use the US dollars to purchase wheat to ship to their factory in Costa Rica.

T-Bills

A T-bill is a short-term debt instrument issued by the US government. The interest rate they pay varies based on the level of interest rates set by the Federal Reserve. They are considered one of the safest investments possible. People, companies, and countries buy them to store their cash, much like a very short-term certificate of deposit (CD) at a local bank.

ZERO-BASED FUTURES DAY TRADING

As a day trader, you can trade futures using large amounts of margin, which can amplify your trading profits with each trade. Futures accounts are zero-based with profitable and losing trades being settled at the end of each trading day. This means losses will be subtracted from your account and placed in the winner's account, and the traders holding the losing end of your winning trades will add to your account. This will effectively decrease or increase your buying power the next day, so winning trades can be compounded by buying more contracts if there is a momentum to the market. This zero-based account settling coupled with high margin can lead to highly profitable trading days. Futures day trading is commonly used by high frequency, algorithmic-driven hedge funds (CTAs) to capture very high returns.

Downsides of day trading futures include large account minimums and large contract sizes. Some of the financial futures contracts can be as large as $1 million per contract, which can be a barrier for even seasoned day traders. Additionally, the futures markets are usually opened in the mornings and closed by early afternoon. This limits your ability to trade futures if you are building up skills while holding a full-time job.

STARTING TO TRADE

Information Sources and News Feeds

While there are many places to look for trading ideas, you should focus on two: trusted sources and market chatter. Trusted sources will tell you the most likely future direction of the market. Market chatter can be useful, but only after careful analysis.

TRUSTED SOURCES

A solid place to start are the longer-term reports and market summaries that are published by your broker. Market reports and summaries offer a logical view of the market and historical context through which you can build your long-term knowledge base. They are often based on mathematics, past market activity, market fundamentals, and technical indicators. These longer reports should be read during times when you are not trading. You should study them for content and absorb the themes the analysts are presenting. Look for repeating patterns and become familiar with the language. For example, the report might say that there should be a "more cautious stance taken in the market overall for the next few weeks." Always ask why this is the case; you might learn that the S&P 500 has entered into an overbought range. This means that according to fundamentals, the stocks in it have risen in price to a point where further increases will be harder to achieve, and the chances of the index falling or moving sideways for a while are higher than normal. Sometimes, these stocks may have an overall high average P/E (price/earnings ratio), meaning the prices of the stocks are too high compared to the estimated earnings of the companies. Also, the report might state that the S&P 500 has been sitting near a resistance level for a week, unable to breach an important level. Resistance levels are price levels above which stocks, indexes, and other financial instruments are having trouble rising. On a mechanical level, it means that there are more sellers than buyers at that price point. Taken together, those two pieces of information tell you that the S&P 500 is near its top and will be there for a while. In fact, it might enter into a stall, or worse, a correction (when an overvalued market is sold off to more realistic levels). Generally, it's best for you to understand how the analyst writing the report arrived at the conclusion. The reports are the starting point of your knowledge, and your goal should be to determine these important developments on your own as you learn.

Find the Right Firm

Brokerages usually specialize in providing services to either individual day traders or to institutional day traders. Firms focused on individual day traders will offer more explanations in their reports, both on the fundamental and technical sides. They have a more education-minded goal than the institutional-focused firms. Look for samples of a firm's reports to determine its bias.

Based on the overbought nature of the market, you would know that it is a good time to have or consider a short position in the market; that is, there's a good chance the market will move down at some point in the future and you would like to prepare in order to capture this movement.

MARKET CHATTER

The next place you can look for ideas is the short-term news reports, commonly called market chatter. Short-term news reports can be posted on stock market websites such as CNBC.com, MarketWatch .com, Bloomberg.com, etc., as well as the short-term news reports that take up the bulk of the day on television news stations such as CNBC and Bloomberg. These short-term reports point you to areas where there may be some market movement. Use them to outsmart the markets. Remember, there are a lot of people reading the same reports and charts, and the market moves in a herd mentality. You will have to decide the point at which the price of the product is over-bought, oversold, or neutral based on your overall knowledge and your own market analysis.

Initially, it's best to use short-term public indicators such as wire reports that provide buy and sell points to determine what most day traders are thinking. Again, reliability and accuracy of information is the key: Use trusted sources only, such as those provided by a full-service broker or information news leads provided as a service with your trading account. Because there is a good chance that day traders everywhere have the same buy and sell points in their minds, you should become familiar with what works best for you as quickly as possible. This will help you put your strategies together and execute your trades more efficiently. Never trade based solely on the guidance of these reports.

Use market chatter as a tool to gather intelligence and to understand the thinking of other market participants. Would you listen to your auto mechanic discuss the time he had a concrete driveway poured and the contractor used the wrong mix and then use the same contractor for your driveway? Use the same savvy problem-solving skills to sort out what information regarding the economy, the stock market, oil, gold, interest rates, and currencies makes the most sense. Everyone has an opinion when it comes to money and the markets. But not all opinions are equal, and you shouldn't treat them as such.

Listening to the Market's Commentators

By their nature, news and Internet feeds have to have stories to fill the minutes and hours of the trading day. Even on the slowest, most uneventful trading days these news stations and websites will deliver news with a heightened state of energy, which can make the information seem more important than it really is. Try to keep things in perspective. Confirm the news before making any trades.

GOOD OR EVIL: THE MARKET AND "NEWS DAYS"

Your first and foremost goal in day trading should be capital preservation—keep your losses as small as possible. Your secondary goal is to maximize your capital gains without becoming greedy. This means that you should always view each trading day and each trade with the mindset that a cash position is the safest place to be and that you will only enter a trade if there is a reasonable expectation of a capital gain (making money). Always strive to preserve your capital and only take measured risks in relation to the potential gain of a trade.

You should enter trades with an understanding that the market will react and move in the future in a way that can be predicted with some degree of certainty. For example, you note that typically the S&P 500 trends in one direction for two to three days and then reverses. If the S&P 500 has been up dramatically for three days straight, then it and the other risk-sensitive trades will be ready for some of the market participants to sell off some of their holdings and engage in what is called profit taking. You also might have observed that when there has been a multiday run up in the market with big gains at the end of the week, traders will often relish their gains over the weekend and sell on Monday to lock in their good fortunes. In this instance, you could look to short the market, buy a bear S&P ETF, or build a position in risk-averse currencies.

Remember that if your primary goal is to make capital gains, you are forced to take risks with every trading situation. It would be unacceptable to sit out a day, or to forgo a series of risky trades in favor of ending the day with nothing more than interest earned. That's a recipe for losing money. If your primary goal is to manage risk, you will stay in the game longer.

ECONOMIC NEWS DAYS

Economic reports are held in great secrecy before they are announced. Brokerage firms, television news commentaries, and online forums will have predictions and statements as to what the market thinks the report will say. These predictions are known as consensus estimates and are used as reaction benchmarks by the market. These estimates usually shape the market's response to the news and set the trading tone for the day or longer.

When the economic report comes out and it is different from what the market expected, the market will move up or down according to how accurate the estimates were. If the report comes out and the market predicted it exactly right, the reaction has already been priced in, and the response may be muted or otherwise. In other words, traders built the expected positive or negative news into the value of their trades and positions. Sometimes, the market will sell off anyway; as the event is in the past, everyone knows the actual numbers, and profit taking will take place.

Trading during the various days when the market is reacting to large amounts of positive or negative news can be very tricky, as the outcomes can't be predicted. Since capital preservation is your primary goal, you should avoid trading on news days. The markets will always be there; you can always trade after the news comes out. It is best not to have any positions in your account in the time leading up to the announcements, especially if the positions are directly related to the sector to which the news reports relate.

ADVICE ON TRADING IDEAS

Get Help When You Need It

There is an advantage to having some sort of assistance available when you need it. While the brokers at combination firms usually do not offer advice as to what to buy or sell in order for you to make a profit, they can set a trade up for you that you might otherwise have trouble setting up yourself.

KNOWING WHEN TO GET TRADING ADVICE

Suppose that the trading you are going to be doing for the next few days will tend to be "risk averse" in nature—e.g., you are going to be short in the S&P, long in gold, and long in the Japanese yen. Why would you make these trades? Well, if the market is risk averse, then you expect the stock market to go down. Therefore, your short in the S&P will make money when the market goes down. As well, when the market is risk averse, traders and investors worldwide will be selling their risky assets (stocks and high-interest/commodity currencies, etc.) and they will take the money from the sale and put it into "safe" assets. Safe assets are, among other things, government bonds, lower interest–paying currencies from developed nations (especially the Japanese yen, the US dollar, and the Swiss franc), and—if the situation calls for it—gold.

To dampen wild swings in your account, you could hedge against the risk-averse positioning in your trading portfolio. Your discount brokerage firm might switch into full-service mode and guide you; your broker might suggest a combination of small positions that would be structured to gain in value if the market started to take a riskier stance. Since the Swiss franc (CHF) is considered less risky (and often moves up when there is less appetite for risk), the broker might place a short CHF position with a stop-loss order to prevent any dramatic loss in value to the downside. The combined positions will make money when the stock market goes down. The Swiss franc trade would make money if the stock market goes up and investors look to increase their risk. Because one trade would offset the risk of being wrong in the other, and because of the sell stop in CHF to protect against losses, the combined positions have the potential to lessen the impact of a really big movement in prices in the wrong direction against you.

MORE TRADING IDEAS

Consider reading *The Wall Street Journal* in the morning before trading or *Investor's Business Daily* (www.investors.com) on Saturday to get an idea of what the markets are doing and what big money managers are thinking. You can polish your technical chart reading skills by checking out articles on StockCharts.com. For in-depth articles on trading, you can go to *Technical Analysis of Stocks and Commodities* (https://traders.com). Learn from master traders such as the immortal Jesse Livermore. Even though his biographical account of the markets in the early 1920s, *Reminiscences of a Stock Operator*, might sound outdated, Livermore was probably the first successful day trader and his insights are invaluable. You could even find yourself spending time listening to audio versions of various periodicals, trading books, and podcasts such as *The Bulletin with UBS* (https://monocle.com/radio/shows/the-bulletin-with-ubs), or *Exchanges at Goldman Sachs* (www.goldmansachs.com/intelligence/podcasts).

DWELLING ON THE MARKETS

When you think about the markets and day trading frequently, you will reach a point that you are good at reading price charts, placing trades, and making profits based on your own decisions and knowledge.

You may wonder: Why did the S&P 500 go up (or down) so much in the past week? Or you might say to yourself, *I've had a good first week trading that S&P ETF.* When that happens, always ask yourself why. You might think, *Did I call it right, or did I get lucky?* There is no luck. Figure out the reasons. Research the market's conditions and look for parallels. History does not repeat itself perfectly, but similar conditions in the market often produce similar results.

If you are day trading FX, you might think that the European Central Bank has been behind in raising interest rates in comparison to Norges Bank, the central bank of Norway. Ask yourself, will they raise rates in the near future? Central banks will usually forecast their next interest rate moves in advance. See how the markets respond to central banker speeches. Then look for the best potential trading opportunities through a thorough review of your currency pairs.

If you trade what you like, you'll have better results and you will get to the point where you are naturally focused on the subject of the market, your account, and making money by day trading. Getting to know the ins and outs of the price of your trades is easier if you like the subject.

You will also learn to use your experience as a guide. If you travel to Europe, London, and Singapore, it will be easier to relate to the price of these currencies as you are trading the FX pairs that contain them. If you really like gold as an investment, then you'll know the price of an ounce of gold day to day without any problem, and you will find it easy to relate to this market. Your goal is to get to the point that you think about your account all the time. This is how you will become an expert at day trading.

Seeing the World Through the Eyes of a Day Trader

One day it's likely that you'll realize you've truly arrived at the mindset of a day trader. It may come in different ways; most commonly, though, you'll be driving down the street and see an interesting car that you've never seen. Automatically, your mind will click into day trader mode. You'll note the name and as soon as you get home, you'll start researching it and seeing if it's made by a publicly traded company. You'll learn everything you can about it and you'll look at the price chart and see if it's worthwhile as a trade. That's when you'll know you've arrived.

WHAT TO TRADE SEASONALLY

Changing over the Year

Once you start to study the markets and begin trading, you will notice that during certain times of the year, different sectors have more volume and more volatility. You might even notice that some of the sectors have an overall unidirectional movement over a particular season, meaning the sector will trend on average in one direction for that season.

FALL AND WINTER: GOLD AND COMMODITY CURRENCIES

Traditionally, many professional traders used to take the summer off, so volume picked up in the fall. This is less evident in the present due to algorithmic trading. Robots can trade while the programmers hang out at the beach. Still, volume increases in the fall, and your chances to profit increase. It gets more and more intense until it peaks, and then it slows again around May.

The fall to spring seasons are usually a good time to start building overall long positions in the gold market, either using gold ETFs or gold futures. This is because physical gold buying tends to increase in the fall and ends in the spring. You could also go long on the commodity currencies such as AUD, CAD, and NZD to enhance your long gold positions. These currencies are called commodity currencies because they are from commodity-producing economies. For example, both Australia and Canada are heavy gold producers, and New Zealand is a major producer of soft commodities for Asia.

Not all currencies are cyclical in nature, as most follow no seasonal trend.

Low Interest–Paying Currencies and High Interest–Paying Currencies

Lower-yielding currencies, such as CHF and JPY, are considered safer because their low interest rates indicate that they have less room to depreciate. On the other hand, the high-yielding currencies, such as NZD and AUD, charge a higher-risk premium: They have a greater distance to fall to come in par with the lower-yielding currencies.

FALL, WINTER, AND SPRING: EQUITY-SENSITIVE FX AND THE S&P

The stock market has a bullish bent, usually in November and December, while September and October tend to be down months. During November and December, you can make good trades with stocks, S&P 500 futures, and related ETFs. Certain currency trades are subject to the stock market's ups and downs. If you are interested in trading the currency markets, you could go short on the US dollar versus the Swedish krona (USD/SEK) and go long on the Australian dollar versus the Japanese yen (AUD/JPY) and the New Zealand dollar versus the US dollar (NZD/USD). When the market is falling and there is overall risk aversion, a long exposure in the yen (JPY) or the Swiss franc (CHF) will usually result in gains, as traders flock to the lower-yielding (lower interest rates) currencies at this time. Because currency prices will fluctuate, it's important to monitor the economies and interest rate dynamics of individual countries at any time. Historically, JPY is a low-yielding currency because Japan keeps it artificially low to bolster exports and to keep its economy growing.

FALL AND SPRING: ENERGY

The energy market offers opportunities in the fall and spring. In the fall, with the onset of the cold winter months, the energy that is required to heat homes and offices can present good opportunities for trading. Natural gas futures, heating oil futures, and energy company stocks are good sectors to watch. In the spring and into the summer driving months, gasoline and crude oil futures and oil company stocks offer day trading opportunities.

WHEN TO TRADE THE HOT MARKET

Markets rise and fall based on the interplay between external events and the amount of money that's available to trade them. Sometimes prices move sideways and other times a market—whether equities, a currency, a commodity, or an index—is on a roll and moves full steam ahead. It is during these times that traders all over the world are on the same side of the trade, all trying to buy. This pushes prices higher and higher with each day, and is known as a momentum market.

In these markets, whether in stocks, sectors, or indices, you have two choices. You can get out of the way as the market is on a roll, is moving forward, and probably will not stop until a bubble is created. Eventually the bubble pops, sending the market back to pre-momentum levels. Standing aside is a very safe way to not get caught up in the beginning of the creation of a problem in the market. Markets, sectors, and securities can only expand in price for so long, and when they reach the end of their growth, everyone wants out at the same time, causing a lessening in demand and crash in prices. Or, you can make the second choice.

The secret to making money in momentum runs is to get into the hot security before the bubble collapses. Knowing when to get into the hot market is not as important as knowing when to get out. The peak is never quite signaled until it is too late and the sector has already started to collapse. In a hot market, the best thing is to keep your trades focused in a very short time frame and never have a trade on the books longer than one trading session. This means no overnight trades, no carry trades, and no longer-term, accumulation-type trades.

Don't get greedy. You can trade momentum markets, as long as you get in and get out with your trades, since you never want to be the last one in the trade as it starts to go down. When a hot market is in a correction stage, stay away from it. When the security is crashing, don't be fooled into thinking that you are doing well and getting a value by buying on the dips as you would in a normal market. This type of market is often too choppy to navigate, or too difficult to predict, going down and then up again dramatically and unpredictably. Also, if the sector is falling, it can be tough to know where the bottom is—steer clear of these corrections! It's better to trade in your demo account at these times.

In a collapsing market there are no dips, only lower and lower prices. The sector should be off-limits from day trading and position building for a while. This is true because as there are usually many people who made money on the upswing in the price of the sector, there are usually many more that got burned and lost much when the bubble burst. These people remember their pain well and will be reluctant to get back into that security again for a while—many will never return again. Look elsewhere for opportunities.

KEEPING THINGS IN PERSPECTIVE

The Short-Term and Long-Term Views

When day trading, you will need to learn how to keep a short-term and long-term perspective. You will also need to learn how to use day trading software to get account information in relation to your open orders and your profits for the day. Finally, it is very beneficial if you can use a practice account. It will help you become adept at your order-entry skills and give you a place to try out new trading strategies and ideas.

SHORT-TERM AND LONG-TERM PERSPECTIVES

Frame your analytical perspectives in two time frames: short term and long term. Your short-term perspective should be ultra-short: the time it takes to evaluate the day's market conditions and news, look for setups, and commit to a trade. This short-term perspective will then last until the trade is closed out and reviewed. Things to look for when evaluating a trade include:

- Cash and margin amounts
- Initial and one-third sectional position sizes
- Price-of-entry points
- Overall risk level of the trade

Fifteen-second, thirty-second, and one-minute charts will help you get a short-term time frame perspective. Five-second charts will let you see each trade as the security moves up and down in the market, but they do not show enough perspective of the overall market. These charts can be found on every trading platform, as they are the mainstay of all active day traders and are offered by all brokers.

With a general overview of the fundamental market conditions, you should place a trade with the thought that you will be committed to the idea only as long as it takes to make a profit and close out the trade. Short-term time frames last from a few minutes to a few hours depending on the holding time of the trade. You can have several short-term perspectives as you buy, sell, and hold many different positions during your trading day. Each one of the trades is alive when it is open, and the risk will not go away until you close it out. If you keep short-term perspectives on each trade, you will be evaluating each trade on its own merit apart from the long-term perspectives that helped you evaluate the market in the first place. If you use the long-term perspective to guide you but use the short-term perspective to evaluate each trade when you are in one, the combined effect will go a long way in keeping your day trading profitable.

Long-term perspectives usually involve time frames of three to six months and rely heavily upon fundamental analysis and technical chart evaluations. This combination of analytical methods can lead to very convincing arguments as to overall market and trading conditions for a particular sector. For example, your broker might issue a report that trading in commodities will be profitable during the next six months but especially in the energy sector. You then evaluate the potential for each energy future, energy stock, and energy ETF trade with this overall perspective. Include this sector in your daily review of market conditions to build up knowledge and familiarity of energy securities. You will then be able to use your knowledge and a long-term perspective to evaluate potential trades with a short-term perspective.

Technical and Fundamental Analysis

Technical analysis refers to when the trader uses price charts to predict the direction of the stock or trade. A technical analyst looks at the past price movements displayed on the chart, combined with mathematically derived indicators and overlays, to estimate precise entry and exit points for trades where the stock may trade in the future. He will then use this information to estimate where to place his trade. Fundamental analysis means using a company's financial documents, a country's growth rate, the current status of interest rates, and other facts to predict the movement in a stock or trade.

A long-term perspective also includes macro knowledge of the overall world's economies and market conditions. These are the big-picture ideas: Sovereign debt levels, currency strength, and the role of the world's developing economies are some of the subjects associated with a long-term perspective. These subjects take time to learn and don't often change that quickly. Again, country, market, and sector fundamentals are considered along with fifteen-minute, one-hour, and one-day technical charts (a one-day time frame chart might show the price movement history for the past two or three years).

WHAT SOFTWARE TELLS TRADERS

Your trading platform should provide you with the basic account information, access to news reports, and access to charts with different time frames. You might also see news reports coming across the newswire in one part of your screen and, of course, the price boxes of your watched securities—the flickering from green to red as the security moves up and down in price.

In the activity section, you will see a history of your account including cash deposits, in and out trades, and daily interest payments (if your account has them). As you build up trades during the trading day, the open trades will show on the trades section where you can watch them go from the initial purchase into a profit zone as the market moves. If you have four, six, or more positions open, you can close them out one by one as they become profitable by opening up the close order box and waiting for the last possible moment to realize your gains. The gains will then be added to your balance, to your realized profit and loss, and to your buying power for the next round of trading. With your account software, you can quickly look at your open positions and see what trades are in profit and which ones are in loss.

You can also use the charts to track an open position and get a graphic representation of your trade as it moves up and down. With price charts, you will be able to see your entry point marked on the chart. You can also draw a line on the chart to mark a point that will be your selling point, or set up an automatic alert that tells you when you hit your target price. The graphic charts showing your trade as it creeps into a profit trade will give you a good idea of how the market is moving for that trading day.

Also, when you have built a hedged position, and your hedge has worked well, your trading software will tell you the overall net trade profit in percentages and dollar amount. When this happens, you will be able to close out all of the components of the hedged trades with one click, allowing you to lock in the profits of the trade. Your software will then allow you to review the hedged trade for quality and effectiveness, as it is always important to see why a trade worked well and what can be improved.

THE BENEFITS OF PRACTICE ACCOUNTS

Using Play Money

Practice accounts are priceless. They have the same software and order-entry system as the live accounts. Your demo account will be off the books, will be funded with imaginary money, and all profits and losses will be on paper. These accounts can be very beneficial in giving you the opportunity to try out different leverage amounts, improve your order-entry skills, and try trading in different markets and sectors that you might not have experience with. You can also use the practice account to develop a disciplined investment technique and give yourself a chance to get used to trading and experiencing your reactions to the market's ups and downs without risking actual money.

When you use your demo account to place a trade that is according to your broker's recommendation, you can monitor it over time to evaluate the quality of your broker's advice. You can use a demo account to try out your own investment hunches, and use it to trade when it would otherwise be an inappropriate time to trade. For example, it might not be a good time to trade when the market is especially volatile, when there are uncertainties as to where the market is going, or when the risk levels associated with day trading are inappropriate to your personal situation.

Gains in a practice account will still make you feel very happy, especially when you win a big trade after interpreting the markets on your own, or when you plan out a hedge and it works in the way you intended. Write down everything about the trade and incorporate your observations into similar future trades. Practice accounts help to build and improve day trading skills, gain confidence, and keep your account intact by giving you a way of trading during inappropriate market conditions.

Beware Short-Lived Demo Accounts

Make sure your brokerage firm offers a practice account that remains active during the whole time you have a live account open. Some brokerage firms offer demo accounts that are open for only a month and then automatically close. These practice accounts have to be reopened every month.

Before you begin to trade with real money, you will need to become comfortable with the order-entry system on your trading platform. You don't want to be worried about making a mistake in a trade—going long instead of short, entering the wrong dollar amounts, wrong number of units, or wrong stop levels. Practice will also improve your finesse and confidence for closing out a trade when you need to, whether at a profit or a loss.

It is in your best interest to practice your trading platform's order entry and order closing many times while using your demo account. Start your order-placing training with scalping (trading using a five- to ten-minute time frame) and using small sums of money. Before each trade, write down the security or FX pairs and margin amounts you are going to use on paper before you place the order. This will give you time to think through the trade. You can decide about whether to go long or short as you see the market going. Don't worry about doing it very quickly at first, as speed will develop with practice.

AN EXAMPLE TRADE

You notice that the overnight Asian and European markets have performed well. You could decide to go long (buy) 100 shares of a 3x S&P 500 ETF to capture the gains you think will be in the American markets. You would determine ahead of time that you would like to make a 5% profit out of the trade. After planning out the trade on paper, you would go into your demo account and set up the trade in the order-entry system of the trading platform. You would double-check your order and then execute (place the trade).

Fight Against Stress

Emotions can run high during a typical day trading session. Trading large sums of money in an active and moving market can be stressful. It gets better as you gain experience. Use your demo account to get familiar with the high-pressure world of day trading without the risk of losing real money.

To learn the quick order-entry skills required for day trading, you should immediately open the close order box and monitor the profit/loss level until profit is shown in the trade. If the market is moving slowly or there is time until the 5% profit comes, take your profit early, before your profit goal is met. Your goal is to just get the feeling of making a round-trip trade.

MORE BEGINNER TIPS

Trading in and out in a few minutes with just a little bit of profit will go a long way in boosting your skills and confidence. Your goal is to develop good habits and build on profitable trades. Positive experiences go a long way. Stick to one trade at a time. You may use round lots (an industry term to define one hundred shares of stock or one thousand units of FX) or fewer shares or units, depending on your account's size and your risk tolerance. Develop skills one at a time. Gain confidence with a few shares, get used to round lots, and so on.

If the demo account offers a large sum to practice with (such as $100,000 or $250,000), don't overuse the account, as this will influence your expectations when it comes to dollar profit amounts. If you overuse the account and get used to placing big trades, you will get discouraged when you begin trading with an amount that is less than the amount in your demo account. It is best to trade a few rounds and take a break, since it is easy to get tired as you develop new skills. It is also human nature to get fatigued with making smaller trades for a long time and want to make one big trade for the day and quit. Resist this temptation, as this will not help you. Learning to trade is like learning a foreign language: It is better to have shorter learning sessions every day than to have one or two long sessions infrequently. It's very helpful to have a way to try out new strategies and ideas without trading in your live account. Keep a strategy notebook as a place to write down and plan your trading ideas. For example, keep track of:

- Day, time, month, season
- Overall market conditions
- Level of the US, European, and Asian market indexes
- Price of oil
- Price of gold
- The level of a commodity index
- The price of the major currency pairs

Use your notebook to write down your strategy, its source, and the results. For example, you could write, "Merrill Lynch advises to accumulate long exposure to NZD/USD at anything below 69." Note that today it is at 66, and the market has been down for the past three days. The Asian markets were up 1.5% overnight and now the European markets are up 0.5%. Thinking that you'll try out the theory that the US markets will follow when they open, you decide that a long NZD/USD position will be a good trade. After writing down all of the facts to the setup, you then place the trade in the demo account.

This trade will be separate from all other trades that you have going on in the demo account. Each trade is separate from the other because they were done for different "tests." With this trade, you must be extremely professional and cool-headed about the execution and strategy. For example, if the trade turns out wrong, you should let it ride until it corrects, checking it three or four times that day before finally closing it out at the end of the day, win or lose. When you monitor it, make marks as to the market conditions that led up to the trade, such as "the S&P went down for a fourth day." Do not modify the trade, change stops, or add to the trade in any way.

This is how you spot setups using theory and build confidence by seeing a trade to the end. If there is an unannounced, unpredictable event such as a natural or man-made disaster or unannounced economic statement, then you should cancel out of the trade and void the experiment, as these things were not in the variables of the experiment. You can have several experiments going on in your demo accounts. They work best when you're emotionally vested in the success of the trade. If you plan, observe, and act in a cool, calm, and professional manner, you can learn a great deal. Keep track of the trade, and when the experiment is finished, take notes as to the time in its development, the market conditions that developed, and the profit that was made.

PAPER PROFITS, REAL EMOTIONS

It's important to feel the full emotion of success and failure, and trading in your demo account will let you feel the full emotions of winning and losing at day trading with no consequences to the value of your real account. Experience the ups and downs of the markets, the thrill of the order entry, and the emotions related to profits and losses.

You will learn how to spot setups, how to manage your cash and margin amounts, and how to use a risk management program. When you are using the full educational benefits of a practice account, you will learn how to resist the temptation to close out of a losing trade because you are angry, when to take your profits without getting greedy, how to use moving stops (by using automatic trade closeouts to lock in profits), and when to take a loss.

Moving Stops

Moving stops are a way to continuously move the auto-sell function of the trading platform higher and higher, following the gains in the trade. If you do this, you will be riding your profits. If the stock goes up $5, you can adjust your auto-sell up $5, too, so you will not have to ride the trade back down to its original price if it turns into a losing trade before you sell it out. This way, the trading software will automatically sell it at the higher price, ensuring you a bigger profit.

The more you can learn in the demo account, the better trader you'll be. Consider your demo account as lessons learned cheaply. You should take care of your demo account as you would a regular account: Use care in the trades you are placing. Take a lot of ownership and pride in your demo account and build it up over time, just as you would a real account; it's a measure of your developing day trading skills.

Chapter 5

Handling Risk

Day trading would be very simple if it only consisted of buying and selling and making a profit. In the real world, there is the chance that a trade will go wrong and that there will be a loss. Even worse, many trades could go wrong at the same time, wiping out your trading account. This is the risk associated with trading.

The best way to handle trading risk is to understand it, quantify it, and develop a method of managing it by using hedges and electronic programmed trading techniques to reduce the maximum percentage loss of your account. Risk is inherent to trading, but with a bit of math and the use of programmed trading methods, you can reduce it to an acceptable minimum.

RISK AND CASH ACCOUNTS

The Importance of Real Money

Start by having the right mindset: Think of your day trading account as a cash account. First, understand that this cash account can be used offensively and defensively and second, know how to strengthen it. Do this by learning the mathematics of margin, its use, your account's buying power, and the possibilities of margin calls. Before we get to managing your margin, let's concentrate on the importance of cash.

CAPITAL PRESERVATION AND YOUR CASH ACCOUNT

The primary objective of your trading account is capital preservation. Think of it as a cash account. Because risk offers opportunity to lose money, your account should be in cash all the time. Buy a security only when the situation presents itself and then return to cash. Until a worthwhile trade appears, it's preferable to be in cash, as being in cash minimizes risk.

Each trade should be seen as a supplement to the interest rates that you would earn in the account. Depending upon the prevailing interest rates, you will be earning interest on your cash balance, which is calculated at the overnight rate. In other words, the interest will be calculated to what you have in cash each night and will depend upon how much cash is in your balance and not in a trade. When you are in 100% cash, you are completely safe, and you are earning interest. If you are earning an interest rate of 2.5% a year on a $50,000 balance, your interest accumulation would be $1,250 a year, or about $6.25 per trading day with no risk.

If you were accepting no risk or as little as possible, you would plan ways of adding to this daily accrual with as little an amount of risk as possible.

Hedge Fund Risk

Not all investors think this way. Hedge funds invest all the cash they have in their accounts in US government T-bills. In a separate account, they borrow against the T-bill deposit at a ratio of 4:1. This 4x leverage is further amplified when they day trade FX, futures, and commodities. If hedge fund managers were completely risk averse, they'd leave the money in T-bills.

When entering a trade, you must take on a measured amount of risk. Think of the trading day as an opportunity to add to your account's $6.25 risk-free interest accrual, and you will have the appropriate risk appetite for day trading. Remember, the cash in your account is the source of your salary. Your paycheck from the trading account will be in dollars, and you will be paying your bills associated with the operating of your day trading business in dollars; this is the balance that you should be looking to keep high. Avoid loading up your account with things other than dollars (stocks, FX, futures, etc.) for too long because you eventually have to convert them into dollars to spend.

TRADING AS A SOURCE OF INCOME

You are in the business of day trading to make money to pay for your expenses, to buy the extras you want in life, and to add to your overall net worth. See your trading account as a source of income. Keep in mind that at some time in the future you will convert the balance in your trading account back into money (dollars) to be usable for mortgage payments, car purchases, and living expenses. By doing this, you will reduce your chances of running out of money to pay your bills and having to close your account and your business. Proper cash account management can prevent this from happening.

OFFENSIVE AND DEFENSIVE RISK

Striking a Balance

Think of your cash account defensively and offensively. The defensive approach is to see your cash account as the source of your paycheck and the source of your day trading business's self-sufficiency. The offensive approach focuses on getting into and exiting trades as a way of increasing your net worth.

THE DEFENSIVE RISK CASH ACCOUNT

A defensive mindset will use the smallest number of withdrawals as possible to pay the bills associated with trading out of the account. Therefore, in the beginning, you might take a lower paycheck. Since your prime directive is to get to the next trading day, focus your trading on holding enough cash to get you to the next trading day.

Your account will grow as you become successful, and you may decide to transition to trading part-time before becoming a full-time day trader. During this time, keep your cash withdrawals to a minimum by keeping expenses related to your day trading business low. If you have a full-service broker, they will most likely ask you, "What is this account's primary objective?" Even though your primary objective should be capital preservation, you should answer, "Capital appreciation." This will inform your broker what kind of advice you expect.

THE OFFENSIVE RISK CASH ACCOUNT

When you switch to offensive strategies, focus on entering and exiting trades with the goal of increasing your net worth, regardless of the amount. Trade to increase capital gains in your account on a daily, weekly, and monthly average so that you can pay for your expenses, draw a salary, and improve your finances. Use both short-term and long-term perspectives to aggressively search for enough trades throughout the week and month to meet your minimum gain requirement, plus an acceptable profit.

Trading Offensively and Defensively

It pays to view your cash account defensively and offensively, while changing perspectives throughout the day as conditions change. You might be offensive in the early morning hours as you trade S&P 500 futures and switch to defensive trading after your profit has been made, or if the US markets open and become erratic. With time and experience, you will adapt and switch approaches effortlessly.

YOU DON'T ALWAYS HAVE TO TRADE

Remember, you don't always have to trade in every situation. In fact, if you have been playing your cash account the right way, both defensively and offensively, you can choose to sit out trading days when it is not clear you will make a profit. This way, your account will have enough profit and gains built into it to allow for a day off. Remember, work toward weekly and monthly average gains to avoid forcing yourself to trade in every market condition.

STRENGTHENING YOUR CASH ACCOUNT

View any loss that occurs in your day trading account as a withdrawal—e.g., if you have a balance of $10,000 in your account and you withdraw a monthly expense account of $500 to pay for the expenses directly related to a month's day trading activity, and the same day you lose $500 in your account, you have then made a "withdrawal" from your day trading account of $1,000 for the day. To bring the account back up to its original buying power, you will have to make an additional $1,000 in profits to get the account back up to $10,000. Focus on always returning the balance to the original amount—you should make money each month equal to the expenses associated with trading and replacing any losses you have incurred, plus an acceptable interest rate.

This is sensible, especially if you take a defensive approach to withdrawals by minimizing your expenses and only entering into trades where you have a good chance of exiting with the same amount you entered with or better.

KEEPING YOUR CASH ACCOUNT INTACT

Focus on keeping your cash account intact; keep it safe and ready for the next day's trading. Avoid at all costs a situation where you risk not having enough cash to last to the next trading day! You should enter into every trade with the goal that it will enhance your cash position. Your cash account doesn't just strengthen with increases; it strengthens with security and potential. For example, if you have a large enough balance in your account, you can limit the size of the margin you are using on each trade to enter a trade that has a longer time frame. In this case, you can use more of your cash and less of your margin, reducing the overall risk of the trade.

If the fundamentals and the technical indicators are telling you that the trade is good, the opportunity to make money is higher. There is still a risk involved due to the holding length of the trade; the longer a trade, the greater the risk.

Total Return Strategy

The returns of your account that result from combining interest accrual and trading gains are often called the total return. Think of your trades as the safe trade, the risky trade, and the very risky trade. The safe trade is your cash balance and the short-term, small positions that you will close quickly. These trades will strengthen your cash account the most, but don't expect these small trades to generate enough profit to use as income. Think about the profit generated from these small trades as adding to the buying power of your account through compounding, and as increasing your margin.

For every $10 you make in profit with these lower-risk trades, you will strengthen your cash account by $15–$5,000 worth of buying power, depending upon the margin amounts you are using (1.5:1 for equities and up to 500:1 for Forex).

CONTROLLING THE RISK OF EACH TRADE

Using Trading Plans

To manage the risk of each trade, use written trading plans. Include entry points, expected time in the trade, and exit points. Also, set a stop-loss order and a take-profit order at the time of the opening of the trade.

SETTING A STOP-LOSS ORDER

A stop-loss order is a way of automatically closing out of a trade. You pre-calculate the maximum loss you are willing to take in the trade and set this in the form of a stop-loss order. This limits the percentage and dollar amount of the potential loss of the trade. A take-profit order lets you enter the amount of profit in percentage or dollar amount that you would like to make on the trade. When the security reaches the price required to meet your preset profit amount, your trading platform will automatically close out the position and lock in your gains. Both stop-loss and take-profit orders are key to planning a trade and are good tools to use in effective active risk management of your day trading account.

When planning your trading day, always review the markets while scanning for potential day trading setups. After taking note of the setups that are available, you then choose the best of these and plan each trade before placing the orders.

When you are ready to commit to a trade, call up the "place order" screen on your trading platform. The order screen will have fields for the symbol of the security, number of units, and the price at which it will execute. In addition to these fields, there are fields labeled "Take Profit" and "Stop Loss." As you enter in the number of units of the trade, the trade value in dollars will show as well as the margin used. Before you press the "submit" button and execute the trade, you can lock in your planned profit and limit the potential loss involved in this trade. To lock in your gains, enter the price of the security at which you'd like to have the trading platform close the order automatically into the "Take Profit" field. Next, use the "Stop Loss" field of the order-entry screen to set the maximum amount of loss for the trade before the trade automatically closes out.

Minimizing Risk

You wouldn't take a trip to a foreign country without telling someone where you were going and when you would be back. Tell yourself where you are going with a trade and when you are coming back by setting profit and loss limits ahead of the trade.

RISK MANAGEMENT AND MOVING STOPS

A useful risk management technique such as the 2% rule lets you prevent and control a major meltdown in a trade. The 2% rule closes trades with no more than 2% of your total account balance lost. For example, suppose you have a $10,000 balance in your account, and you have an order on the books for one hundred shares of an energy ETF at $10 per share for a total of $1,000. You would place a stop-loss order at $8 ($10,000 × 2% = $200 maximum loss. $1,000 total position – $200 maximum loss = $800 minimum ending trade value. $800/100 shares = $8 per share). This very effective risk management tool is a great example of setting your expectations before the trade is made by devising and executing your day trading plan. Make this trade after reviewing all relevant market indicators, news, and charts to maximize a favorable trade outcome.

Automatic Moving Stops

There is often an option on your order-entry system on your trading platform to make a moving stop activate automatically: You can set the percentage, pip, or dollar amount that you would like to use. Your trading platform then automatically adjusts the moving stop up as the security moves up (or down, if you are shorting or selling the security).

Of course, there is the saying, "Cut your losses and let your profits run." In practical terms, this means to raise your stop losses up as the price of the security gains. If you place a trade for a stock at $15 and a stop-loss order at $12.50, you are $2.50 behind the market price of the stock. As the stock moves up in price, you would move the stop to exactly $2.50 behind the moving market price of the stock—i.e., if the stock moved to $18.75, you would move your stop to $16.25. This would trigger a closing-sell order at the new price of $16.25 and would lock in $1.25 in gains. As the stock moves higher from $18.75, you move the stop loss higher yet. This is known as raising your stop and is an effective tool in keeping your profits intact in moving markets. Risk management methods such as the 2% rule and moving stops are crucial tools in the game of day trading. Together, they increase your chances of staying in the game.

Chapter 6

Trade Setups and Information

Because you may have more than one potential trade, it's good to start at the top with the big picture and work your way down to specifics. Do this by reviewing the news. Next, review your price charts for confirmation. Then decide what market to trade. Finally, drill down inside your chosen market for profitable trades, knowing that for every potential winner you may have multiple potential losers. It helps to look for divergences where the news suggests that an asset class should be moving in a certain direction, while the price charts say something different. If the price charts don't confirm the news, explore this area of the market more deeply. Your final step is to make sure that your account is well funded and that your margin can handle the trades you're planning to make.

HOW DOES MARGIN WORK?

Your Cash Account's Buying Power

Buying on margin is like buying securities with a credit card. You can buy more than you could have with only the cash in your account. When you have your day trading account set up with the ability to use margin, you can put up cash and securities as collateral in a loan to buy more securities. This leads to bigger trades and potentially bigger profits.

Using margin for stock trading is like making a down payment on a car or a house. In both cases, you put down a required amount and finance the rest. With a car, it is often 10% down and financing is 90%; with a house, it's 20% and you finance 80%. When you are financing stock, futures, or FX with margin, you are putting down anywhere from 2% to 66% of the total amount of securities purchased.

For example, using margin you would need to put down $660 for each $1,000 worth of stock or ETFs purchased, and $20 for each $1,000 worth of FX purchased at a 50:1 margin in a Forex account. This loan between you and your brokerage house is opened and closed with each round trip of securities trading. Thus, your available margin rises and falls depending upon the number and size of trades you make during the day. The brokerage constantly adjusts the amount of margin available as you trade.

Adjust your margin level based on your trading experience. When starting out, consider using a lower margin ratio, as it lowers the impact of a fast market, and raise it as you gain experience. An alternative is to set your margin level at the point that you would use it normally and start by training yourself to place trades with higher leverage.

The margin available in your account rises and falls, as the trades that are open profit or fall in value. Larger accounts have more margin value. Cash plus the available margin equals the buying power of your account. That buying power rises and falls with the gain and loss of each trade. If your trades are highly leveraged, the margin and buying power in your account can move quite rapidly.

THE MATHEMATICS OF MARGIN

Margin acts as a multiplier on the price movement of each security. First, set the amount of margin you would like to use. If you would like to use 50% margin on a hundred-share purchase of a stock ETF, you need to pay for it with two-thirds down and the other one-third with margin. If the initial purchase is $15,000, you need to have $10,000 cash and $5,000 margin available.

On a good day, the ETF that you bought is up 10% for a gain of $1,500. Your actual percentage gain is much higher than 10%. It is calculated by dividing the dollar gain by the actual amount invested: $1,500 divided by $10,000, resulting in a 15% profit on actual capital invested.

This illustrates the multiplier effect of the margin on profits. Adjust the level of margin you use in a trade to fit the amount of risk (volatility) associated with that security. For example, you know that the S&P 500 has lower volatility than an individual stock, ETF, leveraged ETF, FX pair, or commodity (the S&P 500 is comprised of five hundred of the largest stocks in the US markets, and therefore is internally diversified, as opposed to trading only one stock); use higher amounts of leverage for these positions. To reduce risk, use lower margin when trading volatile sectors, such as the technology sector.

The mathematics of margin work for the downside as well. In the same example, you put up $10,000 in cash and use $5,000 in margin to buy $15,000 worth of the stock ETF. The market is having a rough day, and the sector you are trading goes to the downside of 10%. Because you're trading on margin, your losses are amplified much like when there were gains. To calculate the losses, divide the loss amount by the total actual capital investment: $1,500 divided by $10,000, or a loss of 15%. Margin acts as a lever to increase the percentage movement in the stock, ETF, currency, or future.

MARGIN LIMITS

The maximum amount of margin available to use in your brokerage account is limited by the type of security you are day trading. Market regulators set the amount of margin that can be used in stock, ETF, and futures accounts. This is because some of the world's worst economic problems have been brought about by overspeculation in the financial markets. Overspeculation often causes a bubble in the market. This allows greater and greater price expansion in the market until eventually the bubble bursts and the market plunges. Overheated markets and market bubbles have occurred many times throughout history.

Market regulators attempt to control the formation of bubbles by regulating the amount of leverage allowed in trading securities. On the low side, regulators allow 5:1 margin. On the high side, the amount of margin allowed is the unregulated Forex markets, in which the amount of margin allowable in an account can range from 10:1 to 500:1.

MARGIN CALLS

Margin calls occur when the broker or stock exchange determines that the market value of the stocks being used as collateral for margin falls below what the broker or exchange perceives as their value. If this happens, the broker or exchange issues a "call" and traders are required to add additional cash to the account or provide more collateral. If they can't do it, the broker has the right to sell the stocks that are being used as collateral.

For example, suppose you have highly leveraged the purchase of an FX pair, you have used much of your available margin to buy it, and losses put you in a position where you are below the minimum equity in the trade. When this happens, your broker will issue a margin call. Now you must put up more capital (usually cash) to raise the equity level in your position to meet the minimum. Some brokers allow you until the end of the trading day to fund the account, while others begin to systematically sell off parts of your portfolio to meet the margin. Others immediately close out the position when it meets a level that is below the minimum.

A margin call can be disastrous to your trading account. They usually happen when the market is at its worst and the value of your stock, future, or FX pair has dropped well below what you intended it to be. When this happens, you can be forced to sell at a loss, without the time to be in the trade until your security recovers in value. Calls can be especially costly when a position is closed out without notice, as this takes out all capital involved in the trade.

Often a margin call comes when you are not monitoring your positions, such as when you are away from your computer, during an overnight trade, or during an otherwise unwatched longer time frame trade. If you are making highly leveraged trades, keep an extra cushion of available margin in your account. In any case, a margin call can be disruptive to your trading, either by requiring you to deposit more capital or by the positions closing.

You can guard against margin calls through cautious use of high margin ratios and active position size management, such as the pyramid method, where you build trading positions in three separate groups while closing out the positions one at a time. This averages your cost and selling prices, locks in gains, and prevents a large position being established at an unfavorable price. This way, you are getting the average of the price of the trade over time, and if the trade moves up or down, you'll get the average of the prices over the length of the trade, further eliminating the risk that you bought and sold at a less than ideal price.

Other methods to prevent margin calls include the 2% rule and stop-loss settings (automatic closing of a position) to limit the overall loss of a position to 2% of the cash balance of your total day trading account. This 2% limit would, in theory, allow you to have fifty consecutive losing trades before your account had a balance of zero (50 × 2% = 100%).

Margin Calls Can Kill Small Accounts and Make You Nervous

If there is something to fear when you are getting started, it's a margin call. Not because it's illegal, but because it's a sign that you're trading beyond your means. The best way to avoid margin calls is to trade within your means; you should continue to increase the amount of money in your account by both making scheduled deposits as well as making good trades.

LEARN TO TRADE OPPORTUNISTICALLY

Profitable Trades in Any Market

Over time, you'll develop your day trading skills to where you have a feel for the market and plan trades in tune with what's happening. Day trading objectives can change daily, but plan for every position by gauging potential profits and losses. Incorporate your risk management techniques and moving stops for every trade.

GET A FEEL FOR THE MARKET

The thought of your first real money trade can be both frightening and exciting. Before you trade, do your best to make sure you are ready by having a firm grip on where the market's going and how you can ride its movement for profit. Before you trade, honestly assess your financial market awareness. Gain confidence by being prepared.

Monitor your favorite sectors that you trade on a daily basis. They might be your favorite vacation spot's currency paired with your home country's currency. It might be the price of oil or some other commodity that you use regularly. Consider a market index ETF for the S&P 500, the Dow 30, or the Nasdaq.

PRACTICE IN A DEMO ACCOUNT

Before trading, work things out in your demo account. Practice by placing one trade in your demo account for each of the indexes, sectors, and securities you trade and use the notes section of your trading platform to mark them as baseline market levels. Because markets and prices are always moving, you can use the price levels of a sector at any point of your development as your starting point, the baseline to which you make all comparisons.

When establishing a baseline for the market, give yourself time to see a change in the underlying price of the sector. If you don't do this, you may assume that market is always and has always been at that level.

Markets always change, so what seems in vogue during one trading session may be unfashionable by tomorrow. Keep this in mind when evaluating price levels for commodities, futures, FX pairs, indexes, or ETFs. If you watch a sector long enough, you'll see it change in price, or fall in and out of favor, as sentiment shifts. Wait before establishing a position until you witness this change, and get comfortable with each sector's price behavior. Nothing helps you decide to enter a position in a security more than knowing that last month, season, or year that same security was 10% higher or 10% lower.

Long-term analysis of the markets will help you understand how prices can change over time and at what speed. Technical analysis reveals repeating price patterns and trading setups. Without enough time to develop a feel for the market, you will be trading blind. Remember, knowledge of where the target stock, ETF, future, or commodity has been will give you a greater sense of where they can go, whether they're likely to increase or decrease in value.

MAKING A PLAN

Before you place your first trade, plan the trade from beginning to end. When you are starting to trade, you can get caught up in the moving markets and forget your original objective. If you have a written plan for each trade, you will have a record of the entry point, expected length of the trade, expected exit point of the trade, and expected outcome. Writing down the goals of a trade will give you control of your daily, weekly, and monthly overall day trading profit. It will also teach you to enter each trade with a clearly defined outcome. You should know before you open a trade at what point you expect to close it and lock in your profits, or cut your losses. Without doing this, you will get into the habit of opening and closing trades at any point of the market, with no goal other than to make money.

A Trading Goal of "Making Money"

To say that your trading goal is making money is not a plan. Treat your day trading like a business; the capital in your account should be treated as an asset to reach your goals. Meet your target of having a profitable day, week, or month day trading by planning each trade. It's better to have three or four well-planned trades during the day than to engage in an unplanned series of rapid-fire opening and closing of trades.

Many sports coaches teach their players to visualize personal goals during training sessions. A weightlifting coach might tell the trainees to visualize lifting certain target amounts. A gymnastics coach might suggest visualizing a perfect landing after a vault. Try visualizing that you are building the balance of your cash account in order to have a surplus, enough to make a withdrawal from the account at the end of the month to pay your expenses and give yourself a salary. Successful businesspeople patiently evaluate potential investments carefully and rank each one on its own merit and potential.

When a trade is profitable, you can get out of it and generate additional cash for your account. When a trade turns against you and closes out at a loss, you are weakening your account and day trading business.

Get Some Exercise!

Trading during volatile times can be stressful. A good exercise routine can help relieve some of that stress. Go to the gym, play outdoor sports, walk the dog, clean out the garage, or get outside and build a fire pit. Just make sure you get physical so that you can clear your head.

TRADING IN AN OVERHEATED MARKET

Riding Wild Market Swings

The markets often fluctuate, offering unidirectional sector moves. At times, the market behaves erratically. Keep a cool head, as times of extreme upward and downward movements offer excellent opportunities to make money—you can get into trades at the bottom or top of valleys and peaks.

Market emotions come in two forms: euphoria and panic. In the euphoric stage, most market participants share the same good feelings: the market is going to go up, up, up! This is a dangerous time, as euphoria can end quickly. All it takes is one bad piece of information to end the bullish trading pattern, and traders will take their profits or begin shorting their positions. Your goal is to spot these euphoric feelings at their peak and short the sector where they're evident, or even short the whole market with a bear ETF, shorting an ETF, or even shorting an S&P 500 future. Often taking a position that makes money when the market goes down can be a safe bet, especially when all seems too rosy to be true.

READING THE SIGNS

It's imperative to know when the market has reached its top and when it's the best time to include short trades in your portfolio. This can be difficult, but one of the best signs is when it seems that everyone is talking about the market: how good it is, how much money they are making, how this guy they know made a killing in this stock and now is driving a Ferrari, etc. This is a good sign for you, because the trading crowd usually gets into the market at the mid to late end of the market cycle, when the market has been in a good period for long enough to seem an easy, safe bet. So, what should you do? If the market seems to be getting overheated, place a few hedges in your account; keep a tight rein on your stops (don't let a trade go without one!); and use proper hedging techniques. This may mean diversification as well as the use of a bear ETF.

When panic takes over markets and causes very steep declines in short periods, it's often caused by unexpected reports of bad news such as a natural disaster or political problems. These are good times to begin looking for or building long positions in the affected market, knowing that it is often impossible to determine when the change will actually take place.

Building a Position in a Panicked Market

In a panicked market, spread the risk by building positions and modifying the pyramid method described earlier. Instead of using three entry points, enter four to six positions over the length of the market's panicked mood. Use the standard three-point exit strategy to close out the position.

To further reduce risk, take smaller than usual bites of the sector and use the pyramid method, but spread out your accumulation over longer time frames, such as a week to ten days. The goal is to set up a longer time frame trade, much like an FX carry trade that takes up to a month to go from start to finish. You still enter and exit each trade daily but continue to build on those positions during the month. The stock of ETF might be "in play" during a longer time frame, allowing you to capture the gains daily, but at a new price level each day as it gains in value over time. Adjust your strategy to the new price of the ETF or stock as it moves along in time (though, not at the same price it was at the previous trading sessions). In other words, if XYZ was at $75 at the beginning of the week and you were trading it, and it was in play over a longer term, it might be at $85 at the start of the next week (and therefore $82 might be considered a good entry or buy price, whereas the week before, $82 would be considered an exit or sell price at a good profit).

If you are building a position on the extreme dips (long positions) or peaks (short positions), the total return of the positions can be impressive when the market corrects itself. The key is to build the trade so if it goes against you for a while, it will not be detrimental to your account; use stops and limit total margin to prevent extreme downward swings in value.

How can you tell it is a good time to build a position in the market during these times of highs and lows? You will know when the news of the market flows into the daily conversation of the general public and appears in the market websites, whose goal is to get clicks when the audience is all in on the never-ending bull market. When all is rosy and it seems that there is "free money" to be made trading in stocks, FX, and commodities, everyone will be talking and the Internet will be buzzing. When things are going really well, Main Street gets involved, for better or for worse. If the market is crashing, these same people will talk about how the market will never come back. The key phrase to listen for is: "this time is different." This is a sure sign that the market is either at a peak or a valley, people are feeling either very good or very bad, and that it is a good time to go in the opposite direction in the market. Much like doing the opposite of what you feel, if you do the opposite of what the market feels, you can have impressive returns in your account.

CNN Helps

The mood of the market is also known as the sentiment climate. The CNN Fear and Greed Index (www.cnn.com/markets/fear-and-greed) puts a number on the market's sentiment. Anytime this indicator falls below 50, fear is rising. Readings below 25 register extreme fear. Readings above 60 mean greed is rising. Readings above 70 register extreme greed. Extreme readings often preceded major trend changes, with extreme greed often preceding major market tops and extreme fear often preceding major market bottoms.

TRADING IN THE WORLD MARKETS

Using an Offshore Account

You can invest in foreign stocks, foreign indexes, and the indexes of developing parts of the world. This global investing can be done with an ETF in a US-based brokerage firm, or you can open an account at one of the international firms known as offshore brokers. These accounts are easy to set up but can be more difficult to get money into and out of.

If you open an offshore account at one of the many investment houses available, you have to fill out a special tax form and file it with the IRS, indicating that you are the owner of an account that is held outside of the United States and its territories. Not to worry, though, as the form is easy to fill out and can easily be handled by a certified public accountant (CPA) or tax attorney. Unfortunately, this raises your account costs.

Popular jurisdictions for offshore accounts include Luxembourg, Switzerland, Austria, Cyprus, and the Isle of Man. These accounts offer you access to the markets and investment products that are unavailable through a US-based account.

Don't be put off by the thought of opening up an offshore account. Contrary to recent news, they are not illegal. What is illegal is when a US-based holder of an offshore account does not report to the IRS the fact that the offshore account is held by the tax filer.

TRADING THE WORLD FX MARKETS

Some foreign exchange traders use the trading platform provided by their brokers to program buy and sell orders in the evening.

These traders do this in order to trade with the European and Asian market time zones. The Asian stock market and economic news usually comes out from 7:00 p.m. to 1:00 a.m. Eastern US time, and the European news overlaps at 1:00 a.m. to 6:00 a.m. Eastern US time. If a trader wants to get into the trades of the Asian and European currencies, he'll be trading with those economic area news reports, which means trading at that time of the day.

Using their market knowledge of entry and exit points, day traders predetermine their profits for each trade. You can set trades the night before; then, before you go to work the next morning, check your accounts to find the orders executed—you've locked in your profits while you've slept. It is important to keep track of the dates when important economic announcements will be made. You can go to the websites of the reserve banks of the world's major countries and economies to get an overview of when announcements will be made and when economic reports will be released.

Keep It Simple

When getting started day trading currencies, it's best to keep things simple. You can do this by initially focusing on the major currencies, such as the US dollar, the euro, and the Swiss franc. Once you're comfortable with those, you can add the Canadian dollar and others as you gain experience.

Chapter 7

Analyzing the Market

Looking for trade setups is best done systematically. Tried and true techniques of looking for the best time to buy and sell securities lies in two forms: fundamental analysis and technical analysis. Fundamental analysis looks at the internal accounting of a company or the economies of a country, whereas technical analysis looks at the charts of a security and uses past trends to predict its future path. The best approach is to combine both, because the fundamentals tell the story of how events are unfolding, while the technicals confirm whether the market agrees with the fundamentals. If the technicals aren't confirming the fundamentals, it's best to wait until they do before committing money into a trade.

FUNDAMENTAL ANALYSIS

The Big Picture

Fundamental and technical analysis are the backbone of sound trading, regardless of your time frame. Specifically, the two most important catalysts for price changes are interest rates and liquidity. Interest rates are set by central banks. Lower interest rates will usually cause stock prices to rise, underlying currencies to fall, and treasury bond yields to fall (as bond prices, including treasury bond futures, rise). Liquidity refers to the amount of money available to trade in any market. Lower interest rates increase liquidity and are the fuel for market rallies.

Interest rates and liquidity do not tell you everything, however. Reading the fundamentals across the market is very important. In order to read the fundamentals, you must know the economic or financial statements of a country, market, sector, or security. A company's financial statements can tell you how well the company is doing; focus on information on a company's structure, earnings per share (EPS), and P/E. Also, analyze the supply and demand status of commodities and the fundamentals of the world's economies and currencies. Lastly, you should know the shortfalls of using fundamentals as a tool to predict a security's future price.

KNOWING THE COMPANY OR SECTOR

When you are first learning how to read the fundamentals, it is important to find and read as many sources of information about the country, market, sector, or security as possible. You can find out about the fundamentals of a country by performing an Internet search for the central bank and/or national bank of that country. Links to the world's central banks can also be found on the Bank for International Settlements's website (www.bis.org). Read through the documents and cross-reference them with the information provided by your broker. Some brokers provide a semiannual report on different regions of the world economy.

If you are thinking about or are currently day trading a company or sector, you can sign up to receive Rich Site Summary (RSS) feeds about the security as news is reported. Some independent news services also offer this service. Signing up can be as simple as filling out a form and providing your email address. Your broker can also be a source for a market overview and can often produce a monthly sector guide as well. Full-service firms do especially well at this. You can get a lot of free information on websites like *Yahoo! Finance* (https://finance.yahoo .com) too. Additionally, company earnings transcripts serve as excellent windows into the business and often offer useful insights regarding the general economy. Finally, individual firms' literature, 10-Ks, past annual reports, and press releases found on company websites are good sources of specific information (such as a company's cash flow, balance sheet, ability to meet or beat analyst expectations for revenues and earnings, year-over-year growth rates of revenues and earnings, and the number of consecutive quarters where a company has overachieved [4+ consecutive quarters being optimal], etc.).

LOOKING AT FINANCIAL STATEMENTS

When looking at financial statements, keep it simple. Check out the latest quarterly report and the annual letter to shareholders; together, they summarize the business operation in both the short term (quarterly earnings) and long term (letter to shareholders). The income statement shows sales, expenses, and net income with year-over-year comparisons. The balance sheet shows cash, what is owed to the company (accounts receivable), and fixed assets. These include equipment, buildings, land, and vehicles. The balance sheet also shows the value of any intellectual property such as patents and trademarks. Additionally, the balance sheet shows any intangible assets, such as the value of goodwill. Goodwill is the value that the business puts on the synergy of the business—the synergy of the business is how their customers are better served by the company operating as a whole unit, as well as the value of their repeat customers. The balance sheet also shows liabilities, both short-term and long-term debts of the company. The last thing a balance sheet shows is the stockholders' equity. This equity is a representation of the difference between what the company owns and what it owes.

Truth in Reporting

How do you know that a company is being truthful with their financials? All public companies are required by regulation to have their books audited by a licensed CPA firm. Audits are usually reliable, although there are exceptions, such as the financial misconduct of Enron that came to light in 2001–2002.

Pay attention to the company's cash flows. This shows how money flowed in, out, and through the company during the same year as the income statement. The cash flow statement shows how the company sourced the cash needed for its internal growth: it shows whether the cash was internally generated through sales during the normal course of business, through the sale of an asset, or through the raising of cash through the sale of debt or equity stakes in the business.

STRUCTURE

Capitalization defines the market value of a company. It's the share price multiplied by the number of outstanding shares minus the company's long-term debt. This is often called the company structure. The amount of debt in relation to the amount of equity in the company will tell you how conservatively the company is structured; the lower the amount of debt, the more conservative it is. This is because during a slow economy (when sales might be off and the company does not produce as much cash), there is, in proportion, less debt to service. Therefore, the company can make fewer payments toward its debt and use more to pay for other things to keep the company running. A useful measure of how well a company runs its business is the weighted average cost of capital (WACC).

Trading During Earnings Seasons

Earnings seasons (when stocks report their earnings) are challenging for day traders. These generally fall during January, April, July, and October. During earnings seasons, companies can exceed or miss what the market expected their profits to be, and this can lead to exaggerated and unpredictable movements in a stock's price.

The WACC varies depending upon the cost of debt and the tax bracket of the corporation. The lower a company's debt, the easier it can pay its bills. Companies that pay bills maintain a high credit rating; when a company keeps a high credit rating, it can get lower rates on its debt in the future. This leads to even lower debt service payment, making the company even healthier.

Cash flow tells you if the company is financing its growth from its own generated sales, from the sale of assets, or from raising money externally. The best way a company can raise money is from its own operations (or normal course of business). This is shown in the "cash flows from operations" section of the cash flow statement.

The other sections tell you if the cash for the company is generated from the sale of assets, under the cash flows from investing. So, a company's cash flow statement will tell you if the company is raising cash though its normal operations (for example, Apple earns cash through sales of its products) or from the sale of an asset (for instance, if Apple sold off an office building). Clearly, cash raised from selling the company's products is the best, as it measures the company's ability to do business. If cash goes up quarter after quarter, year after year, then that is the sign of a company that is in good health.

If the company is selling off assets to raise cash or produce a profit, this is a bad sign, because what happens when the company does not have any more assets to sell? A company should be providing the majority of their cash flows from operations if it wants to have a sustainable business.

EPS AND P/E RATIOS

Earnings per share, or EPS, is found by taking the net earnings and dividing it by the total number of shares outstanding. If a company has $10 million in earnings and the number of shares is one million, the EPS would be 10. EPS of companies can range from 1:6, meaning $1/6 shares outstanding, up to 1:250, 1:500, or higher. If the company is just starting out and doesn't have many earnings, the ratio can be astronomical, in the hundreds, as the company is not making much money. Sometimes, these low profit stocks (also called "meme" stocks) are at the cutting edge of technology, and their product (while not as profitable as a traditional or established company) may be perceived as the wave of the future, with high demand expected soon. Startups are often in this category, as are high-tech companies. These stocks can be the high-flyers with gains of 5%–10% daily and can also experience corrections of 10%–20%. It's risky, but it's the percentage movement up and down that makes traders love these stocks. Car payments, mortgages, or a kid's private tuition can be paid by trading these stocks day in and day out.

Another method of looking at the price of a stock or ETF is the P/E ratio, which is the price of the stock divided by its earnings. P/E ratios can tell you how expensive a stock or ETF is compared to others in the investment universe. The lower the number, the cheaper the stock. If a stock has a higher-than-usual P/E number, this might be an indicator that the stock has crept up in value in relation to others in its industry sector. It may also indicate that it is a good time to short the stock because, all things being equal, companies in the same industrial sector usually have close to the same P/E ratio. When one is out of whack from the others, this usually means that that stock or ETF is undervalued or overvalued compared to the others in its class.

MEASURING SALES GROWTH

A company's health usually shows in its ability to grow its sales. Look at the sales for both the previous three to five years and the past few quarters. Companies that don't grow their sales don't survive. A useful range is 10%–20% year-over-year growth combined with steadily rising growth in the past three to four consecutive quarters. If you don't see this pattern, something is wrong with the product or management of the company.

Smart Management Is the Key to Strong Earnings

The best way to measure a company's management is by watching how it rebounds from a bad quarter. For example, companies like Apple and Amazon rarely miss the market's expectations. But when they do, they correct their problems quickly and let the market know that things are getting better. Poorly run companies are the opposite, often delivering multiple disappointing quarters until the boards finally act and change the management team.

FUNDAMENTALS OF COMMODITIES AND CURRENCIES

The Underlying Numbers

Commodities gains and losses are primarily related to the status of their individual supply and demand. Grains, gold, oil, and copper often move higher when the equities market is stagnant. This means you can look for profitable trades even when the stock market is seemingly going nowhere and is difficult to trade.

COMMODITIES GROWTH

From the mid-1960s to the early 1980s, stock markets all over the world did not increase in value, but commodities did very well; unlike equities and equity futures, commodities have a limited supply. The supply is in a glut when the world's economies are doing poorly, and the supply is tight when the world's economies are doing well. Historically, developing countries such as China and India use enormous amounts of raw materials in their ever-growing industrial sectors. And while India is still growing its economy, China's growth has yet to recover after the pandemic, thus the market's soft commodities, crude oil, grains, and industrial metals are not as robust as they were in the early 2000s.

China and India retain their large appetite for gold, as this is often a preferred store of wealth for the people who live in these countries. While the supplies of commodities are limited and inelastic, the world's supply of money is ever changing. Money supply rises and falls according to the actions of the central banks and treasuries of nations across the world. The money supply of the world's currencies is increasing and decreasing in waves, and in long drawn-out time frames. For instance, during the 2008 economic crisis, many of the world's central banks expanded their money supplies to huge levels; in some cases, record amounts of money were added to the supply. This led to a rise in inflation in the post-pandemic period.

What does this mean for gold? Well, the best way to think of gold is that it too is a form of money. You can't buy a coffee or pay your rent with it, yet the Federal Reserve has euros, yen, other currencies, and gold in its reserves. Moreover, some states in the US are exploring making precious metals legal tender. Why? Because gold is a currency! So, if gold is inelastic and has a limited supply, and USD and other currencies are expanding rapidly, there is more USD, EUR, JPY, etc. in people's pockets to buy a relatively stagnant quantity of gold available for sale. What does this cause? Lots of money chasing few goods, and people with more money (through the money supply going up) being able to pay more and more for the fixed-supply asset (gold, or other property, such as real estate). The consequence is that the price should rise. Yet, that's not always the case, which is why it's important to also focus on price trends instead of how the fundamentals *should* line up.

LOW INTEREST RATES OFTEN EQUAL HIGHER COMMODITIES PRICES

Low interest rates usually signal a large supply of money. This is because central bankers lower interest rates for only one purpose: to make loans cheaper for borrowers. The central banks want people to both borrow and spend frequently. If a country's economy is slow, the central bankers will lower interest rates until it's cheap enough that everyone is borrowing. People will borrow to buy cars, clothes, houses, and appliances, as well as commercial loans to buy inventory to sell. All the borrowing means more goods need to be produced to meet demand, which then means more jobs are created to produce the goods that are being purchased. Those people who work at Macy's, Saks Fifth Avenue, and Home Depot will then be working extra hours (because of all the people buying), and they will have bigger payroll checks and be able to spend their extra money, too, or use it to make payments on yet more loans. It's a domino effect, and it works quite well, although it can take time for the dynamic to unfold. This all depends on the depth of the recession in the economy, how much money central banks make available, and how fast the banks lower interest rates.

To trade commodities, you should learn about their production, the factors that affect supplies and production, and where their demand comes from. Some are in play during peak months or during peak times of the world economy, only to fall off and be stuck in the mud during slow economic times or during major trend changes (which may last years!).

Always look at the market and important changes in supply and demand. Traditionally oil is in limited supply, with new sources difficult to find. Oil is still used by almost the whole world, and nations rely on oil in the progress of their economies. Natural gas is used to heat homes and process products throughout the world; it is difficult to source natural gas, and difficult to get it to its end user. Yet, electric car adoption led to stagnating oil prices in 2024 even during a major Middle East conflict. Solar and wind power also reduced the demand for natural gas, even as supplies remained plentiful.

During building booms, metals are in high demand; this includes copper, silver, iron, and other industrial metals. In fact, when times are good, demand is so high for some metals that there is a significant boom in the scrap industry, such as the iron and steel scrap industries that make shipments to China. Yet, the post-pandemic shifts in supply changes and emerging technologies proved that the traditional views on commodities can change. The grains and soft commodities include corn, sugar, cocoa, and others; these are renewable, but demand traditionally increases when the world's economies are growing quickly.

COMMODITIES TRADING IN THE PAST AND PRESENT

The pandemic changed everything, especially the growth rate in the world's industrial engine, China. The expansion of money supply to counter the near economic depression of the pandemic led to huge inflationary pressures and central banks raised interest rates. Until this situation stabilizes, commodity trading will present some challenges.

Still, since most commodities are now traded electronically in the futures markets, there are very few barriers to entry, and professional money managers, commodity hedgers for companies (professional financial firms that hedge commodities for their clients, such as airlines and trucking companies), and speculators do the business of commodity trading worldwide via the Internet. And because these markets always move, it may be a great place to set up your trading shop, assuming you're willing to master the fundamentals of these markets.

CURRENCY FUNDAMENTALS

In general, most currencies are allowed to float up and down against the values of other currencies as dictated by market forces. In some cases, the governments or central banks will attempt to regulate the value of their currencies through the practice of intervening in the markets, via direct government or central bank buying or selling of its own currency in the interbank market in an attempt to force a change in value of that currency.

If the central bank would like to increase the value of the country's currency, it sells off its foreign currency reserves and uses the proceeds to buy its home currency. This action pushes up the price of the home currency while pushing down the price of the foreign currency. If the country would like to make its currency go down in value, the central bank increases its amount of foreign currency reserves by buying currency in the open market with its home currency, which it prints by fiat (out of thin air). This increases the amount of the home currency relative to the foreign currency; the effect is to lower the price of the currency. This is referred to as quantitative easing (QE) and was done heavily by the Swiss National Bank and other central banks after the 2008–2009 worldwide banking crisis. The Federal Reserve flooded the financial system via QE after the pandemic. This event, and others related to it, caused the Swiss franc to rise in value rapidly and dramatically against other currencies, including the euro and the US dollar. Since the franc gained so much against Switzerland's trading partners, Swiss exports were stunted, and the Swiss economy began to slow. The Swiss had effectively established a "peg" to the euro, with the result being the Swiss franc moved up and down in tandem with the movement of the euro. In the case of the US dollar's post-pandemic QE, the initial response was a rise in the dollar which was then reversed as the Federal Reserve lowered interest rates along with the QE. The result was a massive increase in US dollars, which eventually led to inflation and higher interest rates.

The Swiss central bankers did their QE without warning, causing the Swiss franc to jump in price against the world's currencies. Currency traders and currency brokers alike were bankrupt overnight, as they couldn't protect their accounts from such immediate and drastic price movements. Many trading houses and hedge funds viewed the event as a disaster. The Fed's actions were not totally unexpected because of the pandemic. But the inflationary spike that eventually developed led to higher interest rates and increased the value of the dollar.

BRETTON WOODS AND THE GOLD STANDARD

Under the Bretton Woods system, the US dollar was linked to gold. The Bretton Woods system was an agreement that was set up after World War II to help the war-ravaged countries of Europe re-establish money supply and rebuild trade between neighboring countries. Exchange rates between countries were set and fixed, and the US dollar was the basis for pricing in widely needed commodities such as grains and oil.

The exchange rate for the USD was set, along with the price of 1 ounce of gold fixed at $35 USD. With this, all currencies were pegged to gold, to the dollar, and to each other. Foreign nations could easily exchange the dollars they had in reserve for gold held in the vaults of the US government. When the United States broke from Bretton Woods in 1971, thus effectively ending the system, the dollar was no longer convertible to gold, and with this, the "gold window" was closed. Currencies worldwide began to "float," meaning their value was determined only by supply and demand—as they are today. It is often very difficult to determine if a country's currency is overvalued or undervalued against another as the currency markets oscillate in time frames that range anywhere from several months to several years.

Purchasing Power Parity

The purchasing power parity, or PPP, is an often-used method to determine if a country's currency is over- or undervalued. The PPP is a measurement of the evaluation of the same goods from country to country as measured in a base currency, such as the US dollar. This PPP level is also known as the Big Mac Index, a term coined by the publishers of *The Economist*.

The Economist calculates the PPP by comparing the cost of a McDonald's Big Mac in several countries. The thought is that the Big Mac is a good measure of PPP, as it is made by using the same commodities worldwide. A higher price of Big Mac in one country versus another suggests that that country's currency is overvalued against the currency of the country that sells the less expensive Big Mac.

THE PROBLEMS WITH
THE FUNDAMENTALS

While using fundamental analysis is an excellent starting point to decide whether to build up a position in a security, the approach has some flaws. First, the information that was used to build the financial analysis may not be entirely correct, or it may be outdated. Second, some of the key numbers used in the analysis of the security may be off, including a company's estimated growth rate, or the estimate of a country's PPP. Lastly, even if the information and the numbers used in the estimates are true and correct, the market's response may be delayed or unpredictable. This combination of factors can lead you to build a well-thought-out position in a security, yet the trade fails to turn a profit.

That said, even though the threat of these flaws is real, fundamental analysis is still a key element in a pro-grade day trading business. Reading the fundamentals, searching for trading ideas, and then switching to reading the charts to look for setups is the hallmark of a quality day trading business.

This process that starts with the big picture—analyzing a country's economy, individual sectors, and security—and is followed by sound technical analysis to make the final decision as to a possible entry and exit point is known as a top-down approach. It's used by the largest and most successful investment banks and hedge funds. It leads them, and can lead you, to a more focused security selection, while enhancing your returns and facilitating intelligence-based risk management. By mastering the art of reading the fundamentals, you have gone a long way in increasing the enjoyment and profitability of your day trading business.

TECHNICAL ANALYSIS

Charts, Waves, and Lines

Technical analysis can be complicated for newcomers, but it's a must-have skill to master as a day trader. Bar charts, candlestick charts, moving average deviations, and specific indicators that pinpoint whether money is flowing in or out of securities help you analyze the markets, look for setups, and identify the entry and exit points of a trade. Some of the indicators tell a story about the entire market, while others are sector or security specific. By combining technical analysis and the study of the fundamentals, you will enhance your trading program.

SECURITY-TIMING APPROACH

While fundamental analysis looks at economic data, technical analysis looks at the supply and demand data (and the direction of money in or out of securities) as presented by indicators. When you are looking at the big picture and using fundamentals, you are using a security-selection approach. When you are using charts, you are using a security-timing approach.

A chart of a security represents a snapshot of the security's price and volume over time. Bar charts and candlestick charts are equally useful based on how your analytic approach develops. Both charts are available on your day trading software or at any one of the commercially available sites online, such as StockCharts.com or Barchart.com.

USING PRICE CHARTS

Some day trading platforms allow you to call up charts and draw trend lines directly on the chart. When this software is available, it is often possible to place your cursor right at the point you would like to make a buy or sell order. This can help you get a visualization of where your trades are on the chart.

Charts can be adjustable as to the time frame they cover. To get a long-term viewpoint, look at a weekly chart, which shows the security's closing prices at week's end. Weekly charts usually show a history of a year or longer and are good for getting a perspective of the price history of the security. For day trading purposes, switch to hourly and ten-minute charts to get an up-close look at the movement of the security in a shorter interval.

Price charts show the highest and lowest price of the session. They also include the volume of the security during that session. Volume is a good indicator when you are looking for support and resistance levels, and breakout activity. Volume-derived linear indicators show you whether money is moving in or out of securities.

CHART PATTERNS AND INDICATORS

Price chart patterns develop over time, and each pattern offers different types of information. Support and resistance patterns show traders the psychology of a security's price. When securities move sideways in price, it's called a trading range. When you draw a line at the average bottom price and top price of the price range, you define the support and resistance levels for the security in that price range. The bottom line defines support level, or the price level where buyers are willing to commit to buying. The upper line is the resistance level, where sellers overwhelm buyers. A breakout is when the security moves above the resistance level. When a security breaks out, more buyers move in, and if the breakout is reached with above-average volume, this indicates the formation of a new trend. When securities break below support, especially with higher volume, the price is likely to drop further.

If there is a lot of volume at either the support or resistance, this means there are a lot of traders using this as entry and exit points. When a security travels past its support or resistance point with a lot of volume, it is thought to be a good breakout. The point of the breakout is called a pivot point and is often followed by a test of the breakout; the market rethinks the breakout, and the security falls in price. The On Balance Volume (OBV) indicator helps to quantify the breakout further. A rise in this line means that buyers are coming into the security.

The accelerated activity when a security reaches a support or resistance level is due to day traders all over the world drawing the same lines. Many of them have come to the same conclusions as to where those important price levels are, and they are ready to react when a level is reached.

IMPORTANT INDICATORS

Technical analysis takes the guesswork out of trading by providing a visual record of the price trend. The price trend is the primary data point, while technical indicators, which are mathematically derived, provide you with important supporting data with which to make decisions. Indicators are designed to help you decipher the major price trend as well as letting you know whether money is coming into or out of an asset.

- **Moving averages (MAs)**, such as the 50-day moving average, help you visualize the dominant price trend. Rising MAs tell you that the trend for the past fifty days has been up. When prices are above the MA, the trend is intact. A sustained fall below the MA tells you the trend has reversed.
- The **On Balance Volume (OBV)** line illustrates money flows into assets. When buyers are overwhelming sellers, OBV rises. The reverse is true when it heads lower.
- **Accumulation/Distribution Indicator (ADI)** is an indirect way to measure short seller activity. When it falls, it suggests short sellers are active and the price is likely to head lower. A rise in ADI, especially when it happens before a rise in OBV, is an early warning that the trend is about to reverse as short sellers are covering their positions.
- **Volume by Price (VBP)** refers to the large bars on the left side of the price chart. These bars help pinpoint important support and resistance levels. When prices rise or fall above these bars, it signals that the trend is heading in that direction. When prices rise or fall above or below a grouping (a cluster of these bars), the trend change is usually more powerful. When VBP bars coincide with moving averages such as the 50-day, that support of resistance level gains further importance.

INDICATORS

Market indicators are visual depictions of price trends and trading action depicted on price charts. It's impossible to day trade without learning to use them, and all traders are different and find some indicators more useful than others. The key is to find the ones that work for you to help you set up your trades.

A good software program lets you build your own customized charts with a few clicks. You will see some of these indicators described in the following section.

The Importance of the VBP Bar

Volume by Price (VBP) bars are useful because they show you where buyers and sellers are battling for the price trend. Larger bars signify important price areas. When there's more than one bar in a price range (a cluster), the price range is even more important. When VBP bars are found near other significant indicators, such as moving averages, it highlights that trading range. When prices move around these key trading ranges, it shows whether buyers or sellers have won the battle and which way the new price trend will develop.

MORE INDICATORS

Price Charts, Technical Indicators, and Financial
Conditions

Combining several technical indicators with fundamentals is the key to discovering entry and exit points in the market. This section covers some of the lesser-known indicators you can use while looking for setups for day trading.

RELATIVE STRENGTH AND JAPANESE CANDLESTICKS

The popular periodical *Investor's Business Daily* publishes the relative strength number for securities. The relative strength of a security is designed to measure a security's relative price change in the year prior compared to all other securities. A relative strength number of eighty and above is considered exceptional. In addition, the IBD Top 50 is a great place to discover price charts of companies with outstanding profit potential, which can be used in daily trading.

Japanese candlestick charts are read much like bar charts. A Japanese candlestick chart shows the movement of a stock by depicting the high price and low price of the security, as well as its opening and closing price, during a given period (usually a day). Day traders use candlestick charts to perform technical analysis of a stock, studying its movements and identifying patterns that signal to buy or sell opportunities. Candlestick charts offer more detail because of their color: rising prices are usually a yellow or white candlestick, while lower prices are usually red or orange.

There are many terms that describe the patterns that Japanese candlestick charts make. Japanese candlestick charts may be too complicated for some. If you find a charting system, ratio, or indicator too complicated, feel free to switch to a chart system or indicator that works for you. Day trading is difficult enough, so keep it simple and profitable.

TECHNICAL INDICATORS

Technical indicators are a day trader's best friend. Even though not every indicator works every time, the study of several can be very valuable. These indicators are drawn from business information, investor activity, market activity, and so forth. Keep in mind that with technical indicators it is best to use several at once, and if they are all telling the same story, then you can consider the information to be good.

THE EASE OF FINANCIAL CONDITIONS AND LIQUIDITY

The first technical indicators involve money supply. Money supply is literally a measure of the amount of money that is in circulation. This includes both paper and electronic forms of money. It represents the cash in circulation, the amount in checking and savings, and the amount in commercial paper—often referred to as M1, M2, and

M3, with the lowest M number representing the most basic form of money: cash in circulation. When money supply increases through an expansionary regime of a country's treasury or central bank, there is more money available for people to use in buying things.

MONEY AND SECURITY PRICES

The amount of money available for trading (liquidity) is the most important influence on trading activity. Central banks are the largest influence on liquidity via interest rates. When central banks lower interest rates, they increase system liquidity by buying bonds from banks, thus increasing the amount available in the financial system for loans and securities trading. When central banks raise interest rates, they sell bonds to banks, which decreases the amount of money available in the system for loans and securities trading. When liquidity falls, stock prices tend to follow. When liquidity increases, stock prices tend to rise.

The money supply indicator is calculated monthly and shows a year-over-year percentage increase or decrease. This number is adjusted for the Consumer Price Index so that it considers the impact of inflation. The money supply indicator is calculated by starting with one hundred and adding the percent change in M2, and subtracting the percent change in the Consumer Price Index. The resulting number gives that month's money supply indicator. If the number is under one hundred, that means that the rate of the money supply is less than that of inflation. Equities' prices historically have remained flat during these times. If the situation is reversed and the money supply indicator is over one hundred, equities generally do well.

While it is important to know and understand the principle of money supply, a better and more practical indicator of liquidity is the Chicago Fed's National Financial Conditions Index (NFCI), which is published weekly by the Federal Reserve Bank of Chicago. When NFCI is in a downtrend it indicates that financial conditions (the ease with which to borrow money) and liquidity are increasing. A declining NFCI usually leads to higher stock prices.

OTHER INDICATORS

The relative value of the entire stock market can be measured by comparing the ratio of the S&P 500 average earnings per share to the percentage yield of a ninety-day US government T-bill. This indicator is called the earnings per share/T-bill yield ratio and can be calculated by dividing the twelve-month earnings per share for the index by the average price of the index. The next step is to take this number and divide it by the current yield of the ninety-day T-bill. The rule of thumb is when the EPS/T-bill yield ratio is above 1.19, it is considered an indicator to buy equities. When the ratio is below .91, it is time to sell equities (1:1.19 and 1:.91 ratios intuitively, but reported as only "1.19" or ".91").

THE CBOE VOLATILITY INDEX

Another measure of the trader's nervousness and subsequent market sensitivity is the CBOE Volatility Index, also known as the VIX Index. It is an intraday index and is mainly useful as an indicator of traders' and investors' feelings about the market. The higher the VIX number is, the greater the negative feelings in the market. A normal reading is anywhere from 15 to 25. During the worst trading days of the banking crisis of 2008–2009, the number jumped as high as 80, showing a high degree of emotional turmoil and even panic in the markets. During the rally in stocks which began in 2023 and was still active as of May 2024, the VIX indicator has hovered around 12–18, sometimes falling below 10.

MARKET BREADTH, OSCILLATORS, AND OTHERS

The market's breadth refers to whether more stocks are rising than falling. An easy way to monitor this is by reviewing the New York Stock Exchange Advance Decline Line (NYAD) every day. When NYAD is climbing, it means more stocks are rising in price and your odds of picking winners are higher. A falling NYAD line usually signals that selling stocks short or standing aside is the better choice for day traders.

What Do Overbought and Oversold Mean?

When technical analysts refer to a security as being overbought, it usually means that the security has risen in price too quickly and runs the chance of falling in price in the near future. The opposite is true for oversold; the security has fallen too quickly and will soon rebound. A simple way to measure the overbought/oversold status of any security is the Relative Strength Index (RSI) indicator. You can find this indicator in any technical analysis charting program you use. Readings above 70 on RSI usually precede either a pause or a fall in a security's price. Readings of 30 or below usually signal that a bottom may be forming.

Chapter 8

Advanced Day Trading

Once you've mastered the basics, you can develop your craft in day trading further. You can use tighter trade setup goals, switch to trading new markets, or even train yourself to trade only on days when the picking and profit is easy. The theories of day trading remain the same, but you will apply them with a higher level of skill. This chapter will help you develop those skills and will enrich your learning further.

LOOKING FOR TRADES

Setups for Higher Returns

One of the most important adages in trading is "Make money by sitting on your hands." This sensible comment reflects the fact that traders can lose money by trading recklessly. Even though you may not have a full-service broker and the structure of your account may feature very low commissions, you can buy and sell too often without thinking through the trades. Even worse, you may trade out of boredom. Entering trades without looking for setups sets you up for disaster.

SEARCH FOR SETUPS

The two essentials for a profitable day trading session are good setups and free capital to commit to the trades. If your money and margin are tied up in a grouping of positions that weren't thought out or were entered into haphazardly, you are likely misusing capital and margin, possibly in losing positions. Your goal is to preserve your capital first, and to have winning trades and to make money second, not to trade for excitement or for an experiment. If you plan accordingly, you will always have available cash and margin waiting on the sidelines, ready to enter a good setup when one becomes available. Always look for the best play of the day before you enter a trade.

RECOGNIZING DAYS OFF

On days when the market is flat and is not offering any good trading opportunities, it is best to continue to be "at work" but not day trade.

Use those days to review your past trades while casually following the markets. Sometimes, if there are no setups in the early hours of the markets opening, seasoned day traders will take the rest of the day off. Their logic is that money that is not lost in bad trades or otherwise used on a flat or bad market day will be there for the next trading session. It's quite all right to not trade during these kinds of market sessions. You're not required to trade each day, and the markets will be there when you come back. Some traders stay out of the market for weeks on end, all the while checking the charts and news to look for setups, while their cash sits on the sidelines, earning interest. These traders trade less frequently since they are looking for bigger gains with larger amounts of committed capital.

Learning to cruise for setups will go a long way in keeping your account's profit and loss statement positive. There are actually fewer times to make really good trades, get in, get out, and make a low-risk profit than there are times in which capital can be tied up in flat markets, or worse yet, unprofitable trades. Trading is a lot like fishing with more than one pole. You bait your poles, put them in the pole holders, and sit at the shore, waiting for a bite. As long as you are searching for setups, you are profitable. Only enter into trades that have good setups brewing, ones that are leading quickly to a profitable situation.

Initially, sitting on the sidelines will seem unproductive, but with time and experience you will see that many of the lower-end, lower-yielding trades go nowhere, never develop into a profit, or end up being losses. It can be a good training aid to trade in your practice demo account when you encounter lower-end trades in a sideways market. This will help satisfy your desire to trade and at the same time give you a chance to learn with a "what-if" scenario.

SWITCHING MARKETS TO GET REFRESHED

Most people tend to rotate among the same two or three securities looking for setups. You might have your favorite currency pair, ETF, or commodity. But you'll find it helpful to switch the markets that you scan for trades once every two or three months. This will refresh you as you view new patterns and study new trends.

Trading the same markets for a while may lead to a typical trader's problem: boredom. You find yourself looking for something different from day trading your usual securities. It is common for people who get to this point in their trading careers to want the feelings of excitement they had when trading was new.

Unfortunately, they sometimes try to rekindle those feelings by increasing the risks they take, especially by increasing the leverage of their trades. When this happens, switch to different sectors or within sectors to trade. This will once again give you the feelings of excitement. You can start day trading commodity futures after you've been trading commodity ETFs. Or you can explore currency pairs with different fundamentals than those with which you are familiar.

Thrill Seeker or Trader?

Which are you: a thrill seeker or a day trader? Thrill seekers enjoy taking risk. They will seek out the good feeling they get by taking risks and will often put themselves and others at risk because of their need for thrills. Enjoying trading, on the other hand, means you take calculated risks and have a respect for the markets.

There are other ways to keep fresh, such as looking at different sources of day trading information, subscribing to new newsletters, or even switching the periodicals that you read. Another method of staying fresh with your day trading perspective is to take a month off. It is often the feeling of being comfortable that allows you to become complacent with your risk management. If you go on a vacation with some of the money you have built up in your account, you may come back with a feeling of having splurged; this alone is often enough to make you take less risk and work harder to make profitable trades. Believe it or not, enjoying the money that you have built up in your day trading account is just as important as building up the account in the first place!

TRADING ENTRY POINTS

Using the Pyramid System

As discussed earlier, the pyramid system divides your trades into three periods, thus giving you three different price levels. It is similar to the dollar cost averaging theory of investing, but each of the three trades is on the books separately, instead of being grouped together.

DECIDING ON TRADES

First, identify a potential trade. Second, go through your risk management calculation to determine the total position size that would be appropriate for your account. Then divide this dollar amount into three trades spread out during the course of the holding period. If you are buying an ETF and you determine that the trade setup will last only a few hours, a one-third entry point would be made at your initial indication to start buying into the position. If you are trading DIA (the symbol for the SPDR Dow Jones Industrial Average ETF Trust) and you determine you'd like to start buying at 130, you would buy one-third of the total calculated trade amount at this price.

Beware of One Big Trade

Avoid jumping into a setup with one big trade. Each setup reflects a tug-of-war between day traders across the globe, which pushes the security's price up and down until it starts to move in one clear direction. Until that happens, stagger your entry points with the pyramid method.

As the price of DIA moves with the up-and-down movement of the Dow 30, make another one-third buy-in at a price that appears favorable. Since the Dow 30 may be moving upward during the trading period, the second and third buy-ins don't have to be at a lower price than the first one. The system is intended to spread out your entry points if the security falls in value, allowing you to have additional capital to invest at the lower price. Three different priced entry points will give you an extra cushion of risk management to reduce your exposure to a falling market. Positions that are broken up into thirds are also easier to enter psychologically. It is easier to emotionally commit to a trade if you know that you have a cash reserve to buy in at lower prices if you misjudged the opportunity for the trade and the market moves against you.

CLOSING OUT TRADES

Use the pyramid system to close out trades as well. Your total position is divided into three equal parts. As the total position turns profitable you begin to close it out in three trades. Dividing the closing out into thirds locks in your profits but at the same time allows for further growth in the gains of the trade. As the trade gains further, the second one-third would be sold off, locking in at that profit point, leaving the last third to be closed out at the next point. The combined effect of buying in thirds and selling in thirds is an effective risk management tool, spreading the cost of the trade over time and prices smoothing the overall cost basis of the position. And when it comes time to close out that position, the pyramid method lets you lock in your profits while offering flexibility to capture further gains in a moving market.

HOW MANY POSITIONS AT ONE TIME?

In the beginning, you may find it useful to have between one and three positions open at one time. This is because when you first start day trading you are learning to identify and interpret all of the market indicators that go into making successful and profitable trades. For example, you will be monitoring the short- and long-term charts and the market news while at the same time remembering the big-picture information, such as overall market trends and security and economic fundamentals.

Limiting your trades will give you enough time to react to all of the market's developments and how they relate to your trades. At first you might find that watching the market develop and seeing it make your positions (and fortunes) go up and down is a bit thrilling and overwhelming at the same time. It takes some time to realize that it is real money in your account, just as it takes time to learn how to feel the emotions of winning and losing trades.

It often takes time to be able to comprehend all the information on a trading screen. If you are starting out and you have too many positions open at one time, you might suffer from fatigue very quickly and have to end the trading session before the exit point of your trades. If you keep the number of trades you have open to three or less, you will also allow yourself time to analyze each trade after it has been closed out. Your goal at first should be to have enough trades and positions open to train yourself on multiple information inputs and situations. At the same time, you don't want to have too many things going on at once. This could lead to missing good trades or suffering from information overload.

MOVING TO MORE POSITIONS

Once you're comfortable day trading three simultaneous positions, you can gradually increase the numbers of total open positions. Remember that when you have many trades open while using margin, you run the risk of the losses compounding into your margin account rapidly.

Let's say you usually trade five currency pairs, commodities (a gold ETF), and equities (an S&P ETF). Your currency account is set to a margin of 50:1, and you are using the following risk management parameters: at 50:1 margin, total FX positions will not exceed 33% of available margin at the time of the trade. You trade the gold ETF and the S&P ETF in an equity day trading account with 50% margin max. You decide to use the additional diversification technique of trading across sectors: one-third commodities, one-third equity, and one-third FX in your total investment portfolio.

With this ratio you are able to have $4,995 in commodities (gold ETF), $4,995 in equities (S&P ETF), and $11,088.90 in each of the currency pairs or crosses per $10,000 in your total day trading account.

This is an illustration of how your accounts would be using margin, and the dollar amount of each position:

Gold ETF 33.3% × 1.5 margin × $10,000 total day trading account = $4,995

S&P ETF 33.3% × 1.5 margin × $10,000 = $4,995

FX Pair 33.3% × 50:1 margin × 33.33% total FX margin available = $11,088.90

MORE RISK MANAGEMENT TECHNIQUES

Managing Risk with Margin

Minimizing the risk in your portfolio can be complex. The risk management is called "hedging the risk." Well-managed hedging gets your portfolio to the point where it can withstand downside risk, while still being set up to capture gains in the market. This section covers further risk management and trade hedging.

DIVIDING POSITIONS

To further manage risk, divide the market long, short, and neutral positions into further thirds. One-third goes into a bucket of market long positions: long S&P ETF positions, long AUD/JPY, AUD/USD, and USD/SEK positions, etc. One-third goes into market short positions: long gold ETFs, short AUD/JPY, short USD/SEK, etc.

The last third is in market neutral positions, such as the soft commodities and grains, and the FX pairs with a market neutral bias (EUR/SEK, EUR/CHF, EUR/NOK, AUD/NZD, and USD/SGD [Singapore dollar]). This would be for further diversifications. As you see, there are basically three markets: market long, market short, and market neutral. Within those three market "directions" there is further position diversification.

Go Short on Gold?

Remember, gold often rises when the markets get rough, or when traders panic. Should gold be shorted? Good question. It is much easier to think of gold as a "safe haven" bet and use it as a form of a hedge against a downward-moving market. Think of gold as a trade you can have to make money in bad markets.

To further manage risk, you can purchase an alternative investment mutual fund that uses a market neutral global macro style, such as UBS's Dynamic Alpha Fund (BNAAX). Dynamic Alpha is a mutual fund that is managed as a hedge fund and has extensive use of derivative overlays to neutralize risk and give a market neutral bias. Consider the addition of an alternative investment fund as a buffer in your overall day trading account, acting to further smooth out peak highs and lows due to concentrated positions. In this position, an alternative hedge fund–styled mutual fund would be held for the medium-longer term, and consist of around 10% of your total portfolio. This 10% will act as a medium-term hedge to your total medium-term trading goals. Remember, while you are day trading daily, there will be ups and downs day to day in your account and even ups and downs month to month. This 10% will act as a diversification tool; professional traders use it as an anchor in their account, spreading the risk and diversifying even further.

PROFITS, LOSSES, AND YOUR BUYING POWER

The total buying power in your accounts will be constantly changing, moving up and down as the value of the trades in your account moves with the market. With higher-leveraged trades such as futures, commodities, or FX, your total buying power will be influenced by the number of open positions in your account and how well they are doing. When you first open a position—buy or sell—you commit cash and margin to the trade. When the trade becomes profitable, more margin will be added to your account in proportion to the amount that the trade is in the profit zone.

The gain in a trade allows you to buy or sell more positions to the open market with the additional margin created. To review, margin is used to buy a position to the open market; as it moves into a profitable position, the gains are added to your account (unrealized gains). Since your account's value is higher, additional margin is available, and therefore additional buying power.

USING A HIGH RATE OF MARGIN

If you are using a high rate of margin in an FX or futures account, the gains you make will mean even more margin on the available buying power. For example: You have $10,000 in an FX account. One of your trades used $2,000 in margin, and at 50:1 the position has a total value of $100,000. As the trade becomes profitable, the gains are added to your account as more margin. If you made 2% on the trade, the gains would be $2,000, and this would be added to your account.

This fresh $2,000 can then be spent on an additional trade at 50:1 or another FX trade with a value of $100,000. The process can be repeated with each trade's gain until you have huge positions built upon higher and higher leverage.

Eventually you can get to the point that your account has multiple positions all built on the gains from previous trades. The downside to this trading approach is that with higher margin, you're amplifying the risk. If the profits in percentages and dollar amounts using the multiple leverage method have been impressive, the losses in the account can be equally dramatic if the market turns against you.

As the prices of the FX trades come down, any positions you have open will unwind rapidly. Your account can collapse under the weight of its own leverage. This is essentially what happens to some major hedge funds and other major financial institutions when there is a shortcoming in the risk management departments. It is a form of maximum profit generation, and when done right for short times (often through automation), it can lead to very high returns. But it can also lead to an account's rapid destruction.

PROGRAMMING YOUR TRADES FOR ENTRY POINTS

Searching for Setups

After you have mastered the art of looking for setups and manually entering into trades, the next thing to master is programming entry points into your trading software. This automates the trading process and allows you to be a bit more hands-free on your trade entry during a trading session. You still look for setups by listening to the news, reading the journals, analyzing the fundamentals, and looking at the technical indicators.

ENTERING IN AUTOMATED TRADES

Once you have determined that a security is good to trade and has the potential to be profitable, you must determine a good entry point. Before this, you were making market orders; in other words, you were entering in the trades at whatever point the market was at the time.

When you program your trading platform to limit orders to open, what you are doing is only committing to the trade when the security reaches the price you've set or better. You can analyze the price of the security ahead of time and determine the best price to enter to make the highest return. If an ETF is at $48 and you determine that you would like to buy three hundred shares at $46.25 or better, you enter in a buy limit order at this price. The trading software tells your broker that the order is outstanding and in place. When the ETF reaches this price, your order will be executed automatically, even if you are not at your day trading desk that session.

Setting the Time

When you program your trading platform with automated entry points, you can set the length of time for which you would like the order to stand. For example, you can have the order be good for the week; if by the end of the week the order is not filled, the order is automatically cancelled. "Order filled" means when you place the trade on your screen, the brokerage house "officially" makes the trade for you, and therefore the ETF, stock, or FX pair is in your account—i.e., you own the trade. There is always a chance that the trade won't be filled; for instance, if the trade was placed when the market was closing. This happens often, as there can be a lot of trading activity during the last few seconds of the trading day. If you are trying to close out and sell out all of your trades during closing, they may not all get filled.

You can couple the automatic order entry with the automatic closing-out function of your trading platform. For example, you can enter in a buy order at $46.25 and a sell order at $48.25; this order will be activated once the stock or security reaches that price—i.e., the trade will fire off, be filled automatically, and remain active unless the order is closed out manually or cancelled. While it is best to remain as hands-on as possible with your analysis when looking for setups and day trading, it is possible to automate some of the process. While you can automate the actual entering and exiting of the trades, it should be your decision as to when and what to buy or sell in your account. Some platforms (especially Forex) offer fully automatic trading. These are called bots or robots and can be purchased for $100–$500. They are usually well-written algorithms that upload directly into your FX platform. They are set to run fully or partially automatic and are programmed to read technical indicators to decide where to place trades. While they are interesting, and sometimes very compelling in their full automation, it is best to leave the fully auto off. A better option is to use it for suggesting trades. This way you can get to know how to read technical charts for trade setups, and you can follow along with what the robot is seeing in the charts. You can learn with an active market and an active computer, helping you indicate when a good trade might be present. Ultimately, it's best if you decide what to trade and when.

There are plenty of companies that promise great returns by offering the use of their proprietary signal service that tells you what and when to day trade. Your goal is to own your account, and to own your day trading profits and losses. It is only when you are making the decisions for your account that you will be able to day trade to make a living.

PRESET PROFIT POINTS

Using Stops Effectively

An important component of automated trading is the proper use of stops. A stop is an automated sell order that is programmed into your trading platform at the time of the trade's placement. An account's risk can be measured in the percentage that the stops are placed behind the entry price. For example, if you enter the ETF QQQ (the Nasdaq 100 Trust) at $400 and you place the stop for that trade at $375, the stop will automatically sell QQQ when it gets to $375, limiting your loss on the trade to $25, or 6.25%.

Lose or Gain Money?

Remember, while it may look as though you are selling out of your position at a loss and losing money, the real purpose of the stop is to prevent you from losing even greater amounts of money if the position moves against you by a large percentage.

If you place all your stops at 10% below the entry price of your trades, you are, in effect, limiting the loss of your trades to 10% across the board. If you are using 100% of your tradable assets and you only have ten positions, you will zero out your account after ten losing trades in a row. For example, you have a $1 million account with ten trades each of $100,000 in value. If you place the stops at 10% behind the entry price, your trading platform will automatically sell out the positions with a $10,000 loss. If all ten trades went bad and were automatically closed out, the total loss would be $100,000 ×

10% = $10,000 × 10 trades = $100,000 loss in total. As you can see, this $100,000 loss is 10% of the total fund. You are limiting your total losses to 10% of each trade with this system. If you continued along with these position sizes (100% of the account with ten trades total), you would have to lose more than one hundred trades in a row to zero out your account (this does not include the trading costs).

Stop losses are a form of defensive risk management. An offensive-orientated risk management technique is to program your trading platform to automatically sell your positions at a predetermined profit point. This will lock in your gain and help you plan how much you would like to make from each trade. For example, you could program your trading platform to automatically sell a security at a price that is 10% above the entry point. This price can be programmed in as a percentage or dollar amount before the trade is placed. The fields in the order entry window of your trading platform would be filled out as to dollar amount or percentage of gain, and you would then place the trade and wait for the automated sale at the profit point.

RUN THE BUSINESS LIKE A CASINO

If you believe that the markets are completely random, are volatile, and are affected by many, many factors, resolve to run your day trading business like a casino. Casinos make money by stacking the odds in favor of the house. If a game table has a 2:3 odds, the gambler will win twice for every time the house wins three times. If you think of yourself as the "house" and if you believe that the markets are totally random and a game of chance (which some believe the markets are), you can set all your trade stops to any odds you like. If you wanted

2:3 odds, you would set your stops to a ratio of 2:3 with the higher being the take-profit order.

For example, you could buy QQQ at $400, set your stop loss at 4% behind the entry price, and your take profit at 6% above the entry price (2:3 ratio). If the market is totally random, you will average an automatic 2% on every trade (lose 4%, gain 6%, equals 2% net gain). To get this system of randomness to work properly, you have to enter many trades to get the averages to smooth out. This is a good experiment to set up in a dedicated demo account.

EMOTIONS AND TRADING

Mastering Your Feelings

After you have been day trading for a while, you will feel the full emotions of winning and losing money in the markets. If you learn how to master these emotions, you can take advantage of other traders' feelings about the market. Just don't day trade when the market upsets you, as this will cloud your judgment. You should understand how to balance risk and reward and how to know and manage your risk limits.

THE EMOTIONS OF WINNING AND LOSING

Money made in the market can give you a feeling of empowerment, a feeling of being wide awake and in control. That's because you're using your mental energy, intelligence, and the electric power of your computer to make money multiply.

Most of your trades will be well thought out, and occasionally some of them will yield very high returns. These high-yielding returns are the positions that have a magical quality—you planned them, but they worked out better than you imagined. Once one of these trades has made a full turn (trade opening, gain, closing, and realization of the profit), you will most likely be bitten by the day trading bug and the seemingly effortless way in which you made money.

THE THRILL OF SUCCESS

It often feels as though the gains you make in the market are making something from nothing. This is why some traders at the big investment banks are referred to as Masters of the Universe.

Not a Capital Gain

Money that is made from day trading is technically not a capital gain. For income tax purposes, money made from trading is categorized as ordinary income. This is because when a security has a round trip (the opening, holding, and closing of a position) of less than one year, it is considered short term, and therefore considered income.

However, you should remember that although your trades are based upon your planning, knowledge, and intelligence, there is a certain part of each trade that is based upon unpredictable market factors. If you keep that in mind, you will be well on your way to having a successful day trading business, and not be trading for emotional gains.

Granted, there are a lot of good emotions that come from day trading and making money; these should keep you trading, but they should not cloud your judgment with an inflated ego and the pursuit of higher and higher risk levels. After a big session day trading in the markets, you should walk away from your trading terminal. Stay humble and you will thrive in the business.

Just as your emotions can be off the charts after a big win, they can be equally low after a big loss, or a series of bad trades that draws your account down. If you have been following some risk management procedures such as using stops, pyramiding, and limiting position size, you should be able to walk away from a series of bad trades with only a bruised ego. If you have been day trading with money that has been set aside for trading and have not been using money needed for necessities, then your low emotional state should outweigh your lost economic status.

Emotions are the name of the game with day trading. Stay cool and as businesslike as possible while allowing yourself to feel the highs and lows of winning and losing in the market.

DO THE OPPOSITE OF WHAT YOU FEEL

One of the key parts of trading like a professional is learning how to think logically when emotions are running high. Sometimes you know what needs to be done with a trade, but your gut is telling you the opposite. If you can coldly separate your emotions from what you have learned and have been trained to do, you can enter very unruly markets and gain from them.

For example, in March 2023, the S&P fell several percentage points for a few days as the Silicon Valley Bank, a major funder of technology startups and venture capitalists, collapsed. Most traders and investors were pulling money out of almost all sectors at the same time, which left a very precarious situation of rapidly falling worldwide markets. If you were a day trader at this time, you might have been very emotionally motivated to keep your account safely parked in cash. If you were thinking logically and were willing to take a small, measured risk, you could have placed a small amount of your account in a highly leveraged long S&P future once the market showed signs of cooling off.

In this instance, the S&P turned around dramatically and gained more than 300 points after a few days of panic selling, and rallied over the next few weeks. This would have given you plenty of opportunities to trade the long side of the market if you'd done the opposite of how you felt the market was reacting. This may seem like an extreme case, but many professional traders will tell you that the market often sends out very negative signals just before the best setups happen and profits are to be made.

Trust Your Training

Often, doing the opposite of what you feel means doing what you have been trained for and what is logically right. If you know that markets are reactionary and emotional in nature, you can learn to exploit the negative emotions that often run in the world of trading. Two of the most common negative emotions are fear and greed. Fear is the emotion that you will lose your money in bad market conditions, and greed is that you will lose out on a perceived gain by remaining in the markets past the normal growth of a position. Using logic and going against your normal feelings can guide your day trading to strong returns. You should be as logical and as opportunistic as possible with the appropriate risk management procedures in place.

Some of the large investment banks and hedge funds throughout the world use this method to the extreme—they attempt to use computer programming and automation to predict outcomes and execute orders using statistics, higher mathematics, and mathematical logic. While these are extreme cases, you can take a cue from some of these methods. To apply pure logic to the world's markets and do so with a cool conviction is challenging. If mastered, the effects on your trading account's profits can be very dramatic!

TRADE WHAT'S HOT

Listening to the Market

You will grow your skills by listening to the market. There are different sources for getting information about the market. How much information, the source of the information, and the quality of the information are important to keep in mind. Whether it is from your broker, television, or the Internet, you should ask yourself whether this information helps decide what, when, and how much to day trade.

EVERYONE'S TELLING YOU WHAT TO TRADE

With finance, the markets, and day trading, there are often a lot of people telling you what you should do. However, market movement prediction and economics are not absolute sciences, and many experts have different ideas and opinions as to what is the best view of the market.

Pressure

Brokerage firms are known to place tremendous pressure on their brokers to get clients. Some firms have training programs that have quotas of $1 million a month in new, investable assets over a two-year period. These brokers will be very eager to land your account. You should proceed with caution when dealing with these types of firms.

Learn to be choosy as to whom you accept as your information source. You will naturally think of economics and the market all the time when the market is really hot and you are trading day in and day out. Your goal should be to get yourself to the point where you are the expert. When reading *The Wall Street Journal*, watching CNBC, and consulting your broker's reports, you must be able to scan for key information that you can use as inspiration for trading ideas.

CONSIDERING EMOTIONS

Remember, you are dealing with the markets: most information sources deal in facts and logic, but the market is an illogical animal. This is because all the investors and traders are dealing with money; along with this money comes emotions of fear and greed. The herd mentality, coupled with the fact that most players in the market are, in a way, placing educated bets, leads to emotional and illogical markets. It helps to think like a professional gambler, with the markets as your huge, worldwide casino. The casino of the markets has so many variables that it is foolish to think that an information source can predict them all. This is what the big quantitative hedge funds and trading desks of investment banks attempt to do: the application of logic, statistics, and mathematics to unpredictable markets that are driven by emotion. When you think of yourself as truly an independent day trader, you will pull yourself away from the information and view it as all noise, but also as an inside view into what the other market players are thinking and feeling.

QUESTIONS TO CONSIDER

When you hear someone talking about the market (or money in general), ask yourself what their motivation is:

- Is the person on the news really convinced that what they're saying is true, or are they just making a statement to fill time on the air?
- Is the article in the magazine really that important, or does that magazine need to have that many pages and the publisher fills it with fluff?
- Is this person overall negative in nature because they had a bad experience, and does this mean you will have the same experience?
- How much of the report you are reading is based upon fact?
- Can this be true?
- What is the researcher's track record?
- Should you care what the market thinks?

If you were a contractor buying supplies and hiring subcontractors for your building project, would you take any plan that was given to you? Would you pick up wood and nails off the street, even if they were free for the taking? Would you ask a dentist to approve the quality of your supplies? The best thing to remember is that it's your money. Have confidence with your views, and be selective with the information you believe.

ADVANCED RISK

Risk versus Rewards

The statement that you must assume risk to get a reward is only partially true. It leaves out the fact that there is a limit to the amount of return that can be gained from a unit of risk, and that often, with diversification, you can reduce risk while enhancing returns. This concept of limiting risk and enhancing reward is called modern portfolio theory. It was first introduced by Harry Markowitz in his 1952 paper "Portfolio Selection," in which he mathematically proved that risk could be reduced by the movement away from single securities and toward the inclusion of noncorrelated securities into the portfolio. By correlation he meant when different market sectors or individual stocks or other financial products all move up together at the same percentage or all down together at the same percentage. Markowitz designated the degree of correlation by the Greek letter beta. A security whose movement is 100% in tandem with the rest of the market has a beta score of 1.0. One that moves only half as much as the market has a score of 0.5; one that moves at twice the market average has a score of 2.0.

Modern Portfolio Theory

Modern portfolio theory (MPT) is based on many assumptions: one of these is that the correlations among assets will be fixed and constant forever. This part of MPT was challenged during the banking crisis of 2008–2009 when most of the world's markets and asset classes' betas became correlated with each other, causing many traders and investors to hold undiversified portfolios.

VOLATILITY REDUCTION

Think of your overall account value, i.e., all of your accounts with all brokerages, as one big portfolio. In your overall portfolio, you can make the addition of lower beta securities and still obtain a high level of potential return in your accounts. Your positions might include an S&P 500 position, commodities, market sensitive FX positions, and market neutral FX positions. Using different layers of risk "buckets" measured in beta, you can build an overall portfolio that would include high risk, high return, high beta positions; medium risk, medium beta positions; and lower risk, lower beta positions. Using a bit of math, you can calculate your overall account's beta to arrive at a number. The goal is to have a desired potential return while having a beta of 1.0 or less. This would mean that your risk was at the same level as trading an S&P 500 position (often referred to as "the overall market").

The difficulty comes in arriving at a realistic beta measure of any one of your positions. The beta of equities and ETFs are found easily on finance websites; others can take a bit of research and work, but betas can be estimated via proxy. For example, you can derive the beta of a currency pair in an FX or futures trade by looking up the beta of some of the currency ETFs that are available to trade. With some practice, you can make educated estimates for the other sectors.

KNOW YOUR RISK LIMITS

When you are setting up a portfolio of positions or placing an individual trade, it is important to know your individual risk tolerance. If you are starting to learn how to day trade, you might want to "de-tune" your strategies and only enter trades that are lower risk. When you are just starting out, it is important to have adequate time to develop positions and not to have too many fast-moving, volatile, and risky trades open. This will give you more mental room to think about how each trade is reacting to the market's news and other developments.

Limiting Your Risk

Limiting the risk in your day trading sessions can be as easy as using less of your overall portfolio's cash balance, day trading three uncorrelated asset classes, or even limiting your trading times to sessions when only long positions will be profitable.

Keeping your trades simple and being risk averse will make each of your day trading sessions move slower while bringing more comfort and enjoyment to your day trading business. Day trading with real money in fast-moving markets is stressful and filled with pressure. If you can learn to ease these factors by limiting your risk, you will keep your day trading sessions positive experiences, from which you can learn and build on. Don't feel as though you have to be trading with high levels of margin, with unfamiliar sectors, or with high dollar amounts. If you feel comfortable starting with minimal risk at the cost of smaller returns, then this system is good for you. Once you are comfortable analyzing market news, studying the fundamentals, reading the charts, and day trading successfully, the next step is to search for higher returns by increasing your risk appetite.

When you are ready, consider higher dollar amount trades, multiple simultaneous trades, or more complicated trading techniques.

YOUR RISK TOLERANCE

The key is to know your risk tolerance and stay within those boundaries. No one should force you to take on too much risk if it makes you feel uncomfortable. You might be completely fine with day trading equities and ETFs. In fact, you might be so pleased with your returns for the amount of risk you are taking that you may never want to venture into the world of commodities, futures, or FX. And, that's just fine.

Don't think that you are not a real day trader just because you have adjusted your risk level to the point that you are enjoying your business, making money, and are generally pleased with your results. Just because others seem to be suffering with their day trading efforts doesn't mean that they are more of a day trader than you. It may, in fact, be that the others who are having problems are expecting too much out of day trading; they may be trying complicated prepackaged commercial systems or attempting to squeeze too much profit out of a too small account.

Day trading should enhance your life, be enjoyable, and deliver intellectual stimulation and profits. It should not turn your world into a complicated mess of struggling with placing trades and then worrying about the potential effect on your account (and mental well-being!). Keep it small and simple, and then if it makes sense, build up into a more risk-oriented structure in your account.

QUICK TRADING

Scalping and Swatting

There are different types of day trading, and all are designed to make a profit, but they differ in the length of time each trade takes and how much of the account will be used. For example, scalping is a trading technique of moving small amounts of money into and out of trades very quickly, with the average trade lasting ten minutes or less. It is best done with three to five positions open at any time with the aim of gently gaining little by little throughout the trading period. It can be a casual way to spend the evening, as you can trade FX on your laptop while watching the evening news. With even the smallest account balances, scalping can be fun and profitable. Commit 5% or less of your total buying power to each trade; with five or six positions open, you should not exceed 33% of your total buying power at any one time.

Regulating Scalping

When it comes to trading, some brokerage firms have strict guidelines in place to regulate the effect of large dollar amounts of scalping, as excessive scalping distorts orderly price discovery. If you plan on doing any amount of this type of trading, check first with your potential broker.

You can switch from each chart showing the different securities you are watching, but make sure you are looking at very short time frame charts: check out a five-minute chart for a trend overview, then switch to fifteen or thirty seconds after you are in the trade.

HOW TO PLACE THE TRADE

The best bet is to open the "place order" box and move it off to the side of your screen to make room for the charts. Watch the fifteen- or thirty-second chart to show that trading has slowed and that the market is taking a breather. Next, get the trade ready to go, including number of units, leverage ratio, and long or short. Put your cursor over the "place trade" button.

What you are waiting for is the security to move suddenly away from the point at which the trade was resting: you want to place the trade at the beginning of the movement and close out of it at the end of the movement. These will be your setups, and although most setups use fundamentals as well as technicals, you won't use them in this type of trading. You are just looking to capture the short-term movements, regardless of the overall fundamental or technical indicators. Go in and out within minutes with small amounts of money: it is a safe, fun, and quick way to earn extra returns for your account, and over the course of the time it takes to watch a few movies, you could add up some real earnings.

SHORT-TIME LENGTH "SQUAT" TRADES

The shorter the time length that you are in the trade, the lower the expected percentage movement of the security is. When you get to very short-term trades of a few minutes, securities do not have much time to move dramatically in any direction. To compensate for the small percentage movements that happen in ultra-short time frames, commit larger amounts of margin and dollars to the trades.

These ultra-short trades can be thought of as a weight lifter squatting while lifting a barbell over his head. The weight lifted in a squat is very heavy, and it is hoisted over the athlete's head in a short, quick, clean-jerking movement. The goal of the squat is to lift the heavy weight only once: squatting is not an endurance sport. If you have this perspective in mind, you will load on more than the usual amount of margin and money (the heavy weight) with the intention of getting out of the trade after a slight upward movement in the security. If the amount you have in the trade is large enough, you can close out the trade very quickly and still make a good profit.

It is true that this type of trading leads to a situation in which large amounts of your capital are tied up in one or two trades. This indeed goes against the usually recommended risk management techniques of using smaller amounts of capital per trade and diversification of positions across securities, sectors, and market bias.

You can use a modified form of risk management when using the high-dollar/margin trades. This risk management includes only having one or two trades open at the same time and using tight stops.

How Much of My Total Margin/Cash Should I Use on Short-Term Trades?

Your combined margin/cash amount for all your ultra-short-term trades should be no more than one-third of your total amounts of margin/cash available. If you have $10,000 in your account, have no more than $3,300 committed to anywhere from one to three positions in this type of trading.

The use of tight stops means that you've programmed your trading platform to close out the trade when the price of the security is very close to the buy-in price. Both the take-profit and the stop-loss orders are programmed in before the trade is made, and you predetermine the gains on the trade in dollar amount beforehand (after transaction costs). The dollar amounts of the gains can be very small as compared to the capital involved in the trade: You are looking for small, quick gains made in a time frame of five to ten minutes or less.

Markets have a way of creeping along slowly when you are trading in these short periods. Don't take your eyes off the profit indicator of your trading platform when you are doing this kind of trading. In fact, call up the close-order screen as soon as the order is opened, as you plan on closing out the trade soon thereafter. The longer the trade stays open, the more risk that other traders will force the security to move against your position. Because trades move with time, the shorter the time in the trade, the less percentage the trade will move (and the less chance it will move against you at a loss—if a trade is open longer, there is a greater opportunity for the trade to move even more in percentage and therefore a greater chance of losing that much more). It is best to get into a trade that is moving and get out quickly. If the trade does not move, or the market is taking a breather, your best bet is to get out of the trade.

Adapting to the Market

Given the number of potential approaches to day trading, it's a good idea to be familiar with as many of them as possible. Practice as many approaches as you can in your practice account. This knowledge will come in handy when the markets are "choppy," meaning they don't trend for long periods or when things are slow. The bottom line is that you should be able to adapt to market conditions.

Remember, the shorter time frame of this type of trade will reduce (though not eliminate) your risk. If the trade doesn't perform in a few minutes, exit it: the only thing you will lose is the transaction cost of the trade. This is a small price to pay for being risk averse with your account.

TRADING OVERNIGHT OR LONGER

Working in Overseas Markets

Normally with day trading, your account starts with 100% cash at the beginning of the trading session and is back in 100% cash by the end of the trading session. However, there is a different type of trading that involves the overnight markets, usually in futures and FX accounts. To trade overnight, look at the developments in the markets that are open on the other side of the world.

You can get some good news and indicators as to what the developments will be in the Asian and European markets from late in the night. To trade overnight effectively, program your buy and sell orders into your trading platform in the evening. The program executes the trades automatically when the trade enters buy or sell points while you are sleeping. Some traders make it a habit to get up early in the morning before the US markets open to see if any of their orders have been filled. If you trade using a program, you can find your trades placed, with sometimes both the opening and the closing taking place, and a profit in your account.

A variation of this method involves looking at the developments of the world's stock markets for the previous few sessions and deciding if the world's markets will be up, down, or sideways for the next session. You then buy into the future or FX pair that follows the markets' risk sentiment (meaning a risk-on or a risk-off day) and place a sell order near the buy-in price. You would determine the direction of the markets by the indicators of the Asian markets, which open around 7:00 p.m. Eastern US time.

If the world's markets have been in an upward movement for a few days, and there has been a big run-up in traders' risk sentiment, then the currency pairs that follow this risk sentiment will have also been up during this time. If you check the Asian markets after a few days of the US and European markets being up, and the Nikkei (a Japanese stock market index), the Hang Seng (a Hong Kong stock market index), and others are down, there is a good chance that the world's traders are selling off some of their positions and taking their profits. You might decide to short the risky currency pairs and go long on the risk-averse pairs and commodities such as gold.

Middle-of-the-Night Trading

You might find placing overnight trades enjoyable. In fact, many day traders find themselves getting up in the middle of the night to check if their order has been filled. Better yet, some traders put their trading platforms on "audible," which allows their trading platforms to announce "order filled" when an entry is filled by the platform.

LONGER-TIME TRADES

Longer-time trades last anywhere from three days to a month. This is covered here to help round out your knowledge of how trading works. Your knowledge of day trading wouldn't be complete without knowing the basics of longer-term trading. Remember, day trading is basically a "buy and hold" strategy, but within a few minutes or hours. Knowing how longer-term trades work will help you master short-term trading too. With this type of trading, your goal is to build up a position over time with several accumulation points. When you reach these points, you buy more of the security. For instance, you might have a simple buy-on-the-dips trading philosophy.

This is a very hands-on technique that keeps you watching your position develop. The goal is to have a selling point in mind and a value at which, when the security falls below this point, you will accumulate more, much like in the pyramid method. In this instance, though, you divide your buys into three to five prices, but when you exit, you still sell out with three equal amounts.

Set Your Stop-Loss Orders

If you are in the process of setting up a long-term trade, do not let the trade just sit on the books if it falls below a certain loss amount. Just as with any other type of trade, you should still be setting stop-loss orders to prevent a long-term position from becoming a big loser.

This longer-term trading method is good for seasonal security setups and FX carry trades. Some good targets for this longer time frame include gold futures, gold ETFs, and energy securities, all of which are often good movers during the late fall and into the winter. You can accumulate the energies on particularly warm days when the prices of heating oil and natural gas tend to move downward. This accumulation would be done with a target selling date as well as a target selling price.

DIVERSIFICATION, LEVERAGE, AND TRADING RISK

Building Uncorrelated Positions

Position building and risk management techniques go hand in hand. You can take steps to limit and control the amount of risk you are taking with each trade and each position. A popular method of building a position while limiting risk is the use of the pyramid method. After you are in the trade, effective uses of stop losses and take-profit stops will help you quantify and limit the amount of loss possible on a trade, all the while locking in the profit target of the position.

VALUING THE TRADE AND BUILDING POSITIONS

When you are thinking about entering a trade, remember that you are buying the cheaper end of the trade. This means that the product you are in, whether cash, a stock, ETF, or future, is more expensive than the product you are buying. For example, if you are in cash and you are thinking of buying a stock, then the cash is priced higher relative to the price of the stock. If you have a stock that you are thinking of selling, then cash is priced lower than the stock. In other words, when selling stock, cash is a better value than the stock. It is the cheaper end of the trade.

Which End Is Cheaper?

To find out which end of the trade is cheaper, you need to know quite a bit about security analysis, including fundamental analysis and technical analysis. Often, though, when trading a security for a long time, you will develop a gut feeling of what is the cheaper end of the trade.

Ask yourself: What's the better value, the cash or the stock (or ETF, etc.)? When thinking of entering a currency pair, you should ask yourself which currency is the better value (which is cheap, and which is expensive?). By answering this question, you will avoid getting into a position that is at the top of its value against what you are selling. Buying the cheaper end of the trade is a good system to help you decide if a trade is worth getting into, and when to reverse the trade and go back into cash.

LIMITING POSITION SIZE

The use of risk management can be a very effective tool to keep your account intact, even after a series of bad trades. The best system is one of limiting position size, limiting concentrated positions within industry sectors, and using stops effectively. The goal of effective risk management is to develop a system of using a bit of math to get your positions built and closed in a profitable way while minimizing the chance of losing money. While the market can turn against you, and trades can go bad, you can follow some steps to limit losses.

The first method is to limit position size. This is true if you are using an equity broker, an FX broker, or a futures broker with or without margins. Think of your total amount of available trading value to be no more than 20% in one position. If you have an account with a $50,000 value, and you use one-half margin, you will have a buying power of $75,000. If it is your normal procedure to use 50% of your buying power at any one time, the total amount you can have for one position is $75,000 × 50% = $37,500 × 20% = $7,500.

Risk Management

Risk management is often one of the most misunderstood departments in an investment bank. In a big investment bank, there are all sorts of traders who are building positions in their own sectors. The risk management function of the bank sometimes acts as the police, preventing any excessive buildup of a position across the company.

This 20% rule is a good method to force you to diversify your positions to no less than five positions at any one time. This diversification between securities will go a long way in keeping your account intact. Twenty percent is the high end of the position size rule, and a drop in the percentage to 15%–10% will further enhance the diversification of your day trading portfolio.

LIMIT CONCENTRATED POSITIONS

In addition to limiting position size and therefore diversifying the securities you are trading in, you should limit concentrated positions by diversifying across industry sectors, or even products. This can be achieved by bundling all your positions in each industry, such as energy, metals, financials, retail, etc., as one position. This makes sense because there is a good chance that most of the securities within an industry will rise or fall in tandem according to the market's movements.

If you are in three positions in the banking sector, enhance your risk management by bundling these together as one position. A second level of risk management would be to bundle the markets in which the securities trade, such as equities, commodities, or FX.

Remember, you are trying to get a snapshot of your overall risk and trying to quantify the overall uncorrelated diversification of your entire day trading portfolio. The uncorrelated diversification of your day trading portfolio is when you have different positions spread across many securities, industries, and markets, so that when one trade turns bad, it is supported by many others that are not related or affected by that trading/market event or news.

LEVERAGE AND TRADING RISK

Actual Returns and Potential Trades

When thinking of the returns you can accrue from day trading, consider the returns from investing in the stock market over the years and the returns that you can generate by putting your money in an FDIC-insured CD. Granted, in day trading you are not investing, and you certainly are not saving, but it is good to compare the annual returns of the three. With the FDIC-insured CD, your money will be safe, but interest will creep along at a slow compounding rate. CDs usually compound once a month, meaning that the interest is added to the principal; the interest payment is recalculated after that, and so on.

CDs may pay anywhere from less than 0.1% to 5% (or higher) a year depending on the prevailing interest rates. On the other hand, the historical average for keeping your money in the S&P 500 for a year is around 10% annually. With both calculations, the time length involved is a year. When you are day trading, the returns can be anywhere from 0.1% to over 10%, but the length of time that it takes to make the trade is often less than a day. Many times, holding the security to generate the returns may only take a few hours.

The Great Recession

In 2008, the Dow 30 fell by 50% due to the banking crisis of 2008–2009—a crisis that almost turned Wall Street and Main Street into a panic. The index actually topped out in October 2007, as signs of problems in the mortgage market were slowly emerging and finally bottomed in March 2009. In March 2020, the Dow Industrials fell 12.9% in one day as the COVID-19 pandemic unfolded. If only you would have shorted the market with a 2x or 3x bear ETF!

If you are holding a security for a day and you are making 1% on the trade, you would annualize the returns to make a comparable against the returns for the CD and S&P 500 investment. In other words, while the trade might net 1%, this is only for one day of trading. To annualize this, you'll need to figure out how much return you'd make if you made the 1% return for the whole year, just like investing in a CD and holding it for one year. To calculate this, multiply the return by the holding period in days multiplied by 365. If your trade was held for one day and returned 1%, the annualized return on the trade would be 365%. If you held the security for six hours (one quarter of a day), the annualized returns would be 1% × 4 × 365 days = 1460%. If you were in a carry trade that lasted one month/twelfth of a year) and your returns were 20%, your annualized returns would be 20% × 12 = 240%.

As you can see, the length of time that you hold the security determines the annualized returns. These returns are the reference required to make an accurate return-per-trade comparison to CDs and the "buy and hold" returns that are quoted by the media.

Remember, day trading should not be considered an investment: There is a considerably higher degree of risk associated with day trading and the use of leverage, but the goal is to quantify the returns on an annualized basis. Once you have the annualized returns, you can better compare the percentage returns your day trading is making.

In addition to the returns, once a trade is closed out and the funds are ready to trade with again, you will have a higher balance with which to trade, which also means more available margin. This has the effect of compounding your money, but the compounding is done very quickly (within the day or a few days) as opposed to compounding once every month, quarter, or year. The combined effect of the high returns matched with the frequent compounding can lead to very dramatic gains over a month or year.

SOME TRADING STRATEGIES

An appropriate overnight trading strategy would be to short AUD/JPY, EUR/SEK, and USD/SEK. These currency pairs follow the markets very closely. When the stock markets are up, these currencies tend to rise along with the equity markets; when the world's stock markets are down (when the market is said to be risk averse), they will likely be down. A good hedge in this scenario would be to go long on a gold future or short an S&P 500 future.

The goal is to place your trades before the traders in Europe and the United States wake up, analyze the markets, and begin to sell off, causing a lessening in risk sentiment of the markets. If you make currency trades, enter your stop-loss markers and take-profit stops to trigger within a reasonable range of movement: FX trades can move as much as 0.5% to 1% overnight.

This seems like a small amount when compared to equities, but remember, you are using high amounts of leverage in your FX accounts: a 0.5% gain at 50:1 leverage will yield a gain of 25% on your investment. This means you will return 25% on the dollar for every dollar of your actual money in the trade. Overnight trading can be a profitable way to trade the equity index futures or FX, as the indicators can be easy to read through the activity of the Asian markets, before the European and US markets are even open.

POTENTIAL TRADES

If you are buying energies, the target selling price might be in mid-December, just as the temperatures start to fall in the eastern United States. If you are accumulating gold, your selling target might be at the end of the year or even late January, as the price of gold historically moves up at the beginning of the winter and continues until the spring.

An example of an FX carry trade might be to go long AUD/JPY, AUD/USD, NZD/USD, etc., or any combination of buying a higher-yielding currency by selling a lower-yielding currency. Trades such as this allow you to accumulate the interest differential daily along with the upward movement in price between the currencies. The interest differential in trade can add up quickly and can act as a form of downside protection in an FX trade. (The interest rate differential is the difference between the selling currency's interest rate and the buying currency's interest rate.)

With FX carry trades, you are borrowing in a low-yielding (low interest–charging) currency and parking the amount you have borrowed into a high-yielding (high interest–paying) currency. For example, you could borrow the USD and pay an interest rate on the borrowed amount. The interest rate on borrowed USD might be 1% annually. You would then move this money into AUD, a historically higher-yielding currency, and earn anywhere from 3.5% to 7% annually, depending upon the prevailing rates in Australia at the time. The rate you are earning in the carry trade is the difference between the two: AUD minus USD. If you earned 5.5% on the AUD and paid 1% on the USD, you would earn 4.5% annually on your trade just in interest.

Remember, you are leveraging your money anywhere from 10:1 to 500:1 in an FX account. If your leverage were 100:1, the yield on the trade would be 450% on the actual equity involved (the amount of actual cash put up for the trade). Not only would you enjoy the carry trade returns, but the interest rate is also usually calculated and rolled over daily with FX accounts, even on weekends. Interest is compounded daily, too, weekends included.

Chapter 9

Managing Your Accounts and Profits

After you've day traded for a while, you might want to make it a full- or part-time job. Part-time day trading can be very profitable and can allow you to have a full-time regular job—this can lessen the strain of trading, as well as give you the chance to learn the business at a slower, more comfortable pace. Full-time trading, on the other hand, can be very lucrative and can offer you independence, much like owning your own business: you set your own hours, have financial independence, and don't answer to a boss. So, full time or part time? This chapter will help you figure out the answer to that question.

FULL TIME OR PART TIME?

Making a Commitment

Once you've mastered the art and science of looking for trade setups, managing leverage, and developing the skills for entering and exiting trades, you'll need to decide on how to incorporate day trading into your lifestyle. Day trading can be done at all hours of the day, nearly six days a week (seven days with crypto), with the markets around the world providing you the chance to trade full time or part time.

DAY TRADING PART TIME

For a more leisurely way to earn extra money, or a scaled-down approach to day trading, part-time trading is the answer. There are many part-time day traders who hold full-time jobs or are full-time parents/caretakers. Day trading part time is a bit slower and often easier than full-time trading. Why? Simply because the part-time trader is less emotionally involved with their trading account, and therefore can wait it out while searching for the best trade setups. Remember, with trading it's sometimes keeping out of a bad trade that earns you the profit for the day. Staying away from the rapid-fire, got-to-trade mentality can keep your trading account profitable, intact, and not "blown up" by overprocessing and overtrading your account. Remember: To keep an account intact and profitable, you should trade less and trade more profitably.

Less Is Best

It's a fact that most professional traders wish they would have passed on a quarter of the trades they've made on any given day, week, or month. It doesn't take many big wins to keep a trading account pumping out profits. Less is best, as the saying goes in trading.

You can be very successful and profitable with as little as five or six well-placed trades a month. If you limit your trading times to the optimum trading market environment and earn your 5%–10% on each trade once a week, you'll be very successful indeed.

If your goal is to add to the profitability of your overall portfolio holding with only ten trades a month, with each trade being done at the perfect setup, then you could spend as little as five or ten hours a week studying the markets and looking for trades.

Part-time traders may earn a smaller percentage of overall profit in their accounts, but most often this is due to less trading, not less profitable trades. So, trading less, but earning more per trade (and risking less!) is also part of a well-thought-out part-time day trading business plan.

DAY TRADING FULL TIME

If you are looking for a career change or are looking for a work-for-yourself type of career where the potential to earn big paychecks is the norm, then day trading full time might be for you. If your account is big enough, or you are investing a sizable portion of your 401(k), inheritance, business sales proceeds, or saved monies, then yes, day trading needs to be done full time, if only to manage all the open positions, leverage, and risk. Day trading with a big account is serious business, not only because of the money that can be made on a daily, weekly, and yearly basis; large sums of money take a bit of babysitting! Even with a semiautomated or fully automated trading strategy, it will be a full-time job to think through and calculate each trade.

Keep Your Eye on Things

Even with fully automated trading systems, expert traders never really "take their hands off the wheel"—rather, they are at their trading desks early, watching and confirming the machine's "trading logic" behind each trade…even if they themselves wrote the software!

If you decide to trade full time, it is possible to turn your hobby into a very profitable business. You will learn that much faster if you spend more time analyzing the market for trade setups, noticing innuendo in market reports that are published by brokers, and getting a grip on the world economies and how they interact on a large stage, all interconnected to each other's markets. Trading is an art as much as it is a science. You learn to do it by studying this book, going through the recommended reading list, examining brokers' reports, and yes, placing trades!

The more trades you enter and exit (both profitably and at a loss), the better you will become at trading. Remember, the best traders make very educated trades. These day traders execute trades that are well thought out, are well planned, and have the best technical and fundamental indicators. These traders think through each trade before, during, and after exiting the trade! The most successful, enjoyable, and profitable experience is when you can use logic and art to preplan a trade, enter into it, watch it work out in your direction, exit the trade at the predetermined point, and log the profits. Knowing, doing, and then realizing what you knew would happen is the most powerful edge in day trading.

To get to this point will take time as you scour the markets looking for setups, thinking, preplanning, and executing trades. It is the preplanning, then trading, and then exiting the trade at the predetermined point that makes you a professional trader. Those three habits will set you apart from other traders and day traders. The logic and the planning are powerful, if not more so than just a few winning trades.

CHOOSE WHAT'S BEST FOR YOU

Day trading can be full time or part time; both types of trading plans can be profitable if you execute them well. Keep in mind the time you have available, the risk you're willing to tolerate, and the way in which day trading will work into your life the best.

REALISTICALLY LOOKING AT PROFITS

Using Your Judgment

You will know when you are ready to make your first trade when you approach day trading as an enjoyable, profitable, and exciting business. Of the three, your ability to enjoy day trading is most important. By framing it this way, you can move away from constantly looking for the profit rush—that feeling of euphoria that comes about when a profit is made in the markets. This profit euphoria can be addicting, and it can lead a day trader to take on greater and greater risks or position sizes in search of further gains. Ultimately, this can be dangerous for your bank account.

ARE YOU READY?

A day will come when you ask yourself, *Am I ready to make my first trade?* You will never be able to answer this question fully without the acceptance of some risk. Not every day trading opportunity offers the perfect chance to make money. Day trading is not an absolute science. If you have been studying the fundamentals, watching the markets, and reading the charts, then you are ready to trade. Starting with small dollar and margin amounts will take the pressure off your first series of trades and will allow you to get into the markets sooner rather than later.

Checklist for Your First Trade

- Read your favorite and accurate market summary
- Check the daily market news
- Monitor the long and medium time frame charts
- Analyze the trends
- Plan your entry and exit points
- Place the trade

It is important to try to make your first day trading experiences positive. Starting small and getting out of the trades early with even the smallest amount of profit will enable you to have the experience of enjoying day trading on your terms.

Put Your Best Foot Forward First

Maximize the success of your first trade by trading in your most successful practice areas. If you've done well trading Amazon and Apple in your practice account, that's where you need to go in your first trade. Just repeat the same steps which gave you the wins in your practice account. Check out the fundamentals. Look at the price charts. Find the right setup. Define your entry and exit points and your sell stop and pull the trigger.

Rather than jumping into a live account, practice first. Much money can be lost in the first few days of day trading if you are not fully ready for the action, excitement, and pressure that it takes to day trade with a live account. Keep your money safe for as long as possible and day trade in your demo account for a while. Remember, you're taking a long view of day trading, giving yourself the best chance to make profitable trades. If you try too hard and place too many big trades without sufficient experience, these trades could well result in rapid losses. If you are impatient when you start, then you will set a pattern of approaching your day trading sessions in a state of tension, frustration, or worse yet, panic.

EVERY TRADER HAS BAD DAYS

Keep in mind, even hardened traders have bad days. They are armed with their best judgment, but sometimes the market goes against them. When this happens, they sit back and evaluate the risk level of every position they are in. Keep this in mind when you get the urge to increase the risk in your account. This mentality can be destructive to your profit and loss statement. There is only so much profit that you can squeeze out of an account. To exceed this natural profit amount, it is necessary to take bigger risks through larger margins, concentrated positions, etc. This is not good business and not a way to turn your day trading into a career. Start small, manage risks, limit margin, and know your profit and loss points all with the thought of learning to day trade better.

In trading careers, there is no "one big trade." Instead, to make a living at day trading, you must make small, measured profits consistently. If you regularly make more winning trades than losing trades, your account will show an overall profit.

The last goal should be excitement. It can be thrilling to day trade, but you should find excitement in making a living doing it, not because you had a hot streak.

Mastering a sector, knowing a product, following it in the news, and then making consistent money by day trading the product is very satisfying. Consistency measures how well you are taking to your new business of day trading. If at any time you do not feel the same excitement making regular, risk-managed, safe trades, and you want to thrill seek by changing margin ratios, taking bigger bites of a position than you are used to, or getting into exotic products, take a break. When you start having these feelings, you are taking your successes and profits for granted—pride always comes before a fall. In these moments, it's best to take a step back and enjoy your non-work life.

BUILDING YOUR ACCOUNT SLOWLY

The Mathematics of Returns

When calculating returns, look at the core dollar amount that is in your profit and loss for days, weeks, and months, and from this figure, calculate a monthly or quarterly average. The reason you look at your returns daily is because in annualized percentage terms, you might have stellar performance in your day trading account.

If, for example, you are in a trade that returns 2% of the dollar amount, at first glance it might seem small. But when you annualize the returns, the numbers can change dramatically due to the ultra-short holding time of day trades.

If you are to calculate the annual returns on the 2% gain, take the 2% daily return and multiply it by the number of days in the year, 365; this gives you 730% annualized returns. To dig even deeper, take the return percent for the trade, divide it by the number of hours' holding time of the trade (let's say three hours), multiply this number by twenty-four hours in a day, and multiply this number by the number of days in a year (365): 2% / 3 hours = 0.667% × 24 hours = 16% × 365 days = 5840% annualized returns when calculated on an hourly holding period.

Although this is a not a standard method of calculating returns, it provides a means of comparison to a CD even if the returns on the CD are compounded monthly rather than annually.

Bank's Calculation of Returns

Banks and other institutions use many different methods of calculating returns. Most are done to calculate the annual return. When you are comparing your returns to that of other investment vehicles, make sure you are using the same method as used by the institution. This will ensure a comparison of "apples to apples."

This nominal APR is the number that is calculated by the straight percentage multiplied by the number of periods in a year. Although a bank CD or a savings account is not in the same risk category as day trading, it is good to use the same mathematical method of comparing yearly returns between the two. Comparisons of APRs will allow you to judge your performance more realistically in a way that can help you determine the return of each trade.

YOUR TOTAL MONTHLY PERFORMANCE

Your total monthly performance is a more reliable indication of your overall performance than how you do on any given day. Over time the good and bad days average out and show an accurate measurement of performance. To calculate your monthly gross profit/loss, take your account value at the last day of the month, and subtract the value that it was at the beginning of the month. From this number, subtract your expenses to arrive at a net profit or loss. Divide this net profit/loss by the amount that was in the account on the very first day to arrive at a percentage gain for the month. Do the same for the yearly profit and loss calculations.

There are several possible performance scenarios, including:

- Your dollar amount of profit is high, you are covering your bills, and you're earning enough to draw a salary from the gains.
- The dollar amount is small, you are covering your bills associated with day trading, but you are not making enough to draw a salary.

If you are in the second of these situations, focus on the percentage returns. If they are high, but the dollar amount of the return is low, consider the fact that you are doing well and are mastering day trading; it just might be that your account balance or amount of total margin cannot produce higher dollar returns for the amount deposited. Be patient—you are doing well. It is only a matter of time before your account grows to the point of being able to throw off enough self-generated cash for you to be able to take a salary draw.

REALISTICALLY EVALUATE YOUR PERFORMANCE

To realistically measure your performance in day trading, look at the percentage of your monthly returns and the dollar amount of your gains. In addition to these quantitative measures, there are the psychological benefits to day trading and placing winning trades in the market. Reviewing both of these aspects of your situation will help you gauge your performance.

How Am I Really Doing?

Only you can answer how you are really doing. You can't really compare your returns to that of any other investment because day trading is not a buy and hold strategy. You may find a gauge of multi-strategy, multiplatform comparable returns on the benchmark Credit Suisse Hedge Fund Index helpful: https://lab.credit-suisse.com.

Remember that it is very difficult to make consistent profits day trading at first. It might even take you a half a year or longer to learn how to consistently make a profit day trading. In this introductory period, it is important to positively reinforce your skills. Do this by looking at the glass half full. It is impossible to accurately set a goal as to the percentage or dollar amount you will make in any given period, whether a trading session, month, or quarter. It depends on what trading opportunities become available, something no one can predict.

Look for positive ways to view your day trading experience while you are learning how to trade. This could mean being happy with a $100 gain in one trading session, a 10% gain in your account in one week, or even ten winning trades in a row. Use the good feelings to stay motivated and enthused about your new day trading career. Challenge yourself to see every positive experience as beneficial no matter how small. This is a good habit to get into and will go a long way in keeping you motivated and learning about the markets and making fresh, well-thought-out trades.

RECORDING GAINS AND LOSSES

Accounting and Taxes

As a day trader, you will need to keep good records of the gains and losses in your account, along with keeping track of any expenses related to the production of your day trading income. These two numbers will allow you to arrive at your net income. When you use bookkeeping software, you can help your accountant simplify any tax planning they might advise.

BASIC RECORD KEEPING

You will do best when you keep a basic record of your day trading business's money inflows and outflows. A basic record can be a statement that can be kept in a notebook or on a spreadsheet. If you have it in your plans to get an accountant for the formal preparation and assembly of your financial documents, your goal should be to make basic records of the cash ins and outs of your business.

You're required to keep basic records for the preparation of an income statement. Record expenses related to the purchase of computer equipment, office furniture, and accounting and office-related software. Plus, you should record your additions and subtractions to your day trading accounts.

List each cash outlay and income development as it occurs, with positive numbers representing cash income and negative numbers representing cash outflows and expenses. Record the cash outflows pertaining to the purchase of equipment and related costs on a separate line with a description and the amount of the expenditure listed as a negative number. Then take the receipt for the cash out-flow and place it in an envelope. At the start of each week, label and start a new envelope and place that week's expense and cash outflow receipts into that week's envelope.

The notebook is the main checking register of your day trading business. Record everything; even if you're at the bookstore buying trading magazines and you spend money on coffee, you record the day, place, nature of expense (meals), and the cost of the item as a negative number.

If you start your day trading account with, say, a $5,000 deposit, record this in the book also as a negative number, as if you "spent money" on the business. (In fact, it is indeed fair to say you "spent" $5,000 on the opening of the account, as this is an integral part of your day trading business.) Much like a business owner putting $5,000 of cash into his business account on the very first day of business, you will be doing the same: depositing the money in a "business account." In this case, your business is buying and selling securities for profit. It is not exactly an expense, but it is money going out of your pocket, and this is what you are trying to keep track of: money going out and coming in.

NOTING GAINS AND LOSSES

In addition to recording the money flows in and out of your account, record the gains and losses on your actual day trading activities. If you are making more than a few trades a day, the best way to record the gains and losses in your account is to note the net gain and loss from your account daily. Write down the value of your account before each trading session. Then compare this to the amount recorded on the closing of your previous trading session. Any difference between the two indicates the addition of interest that accrued from one trading session to the next. This interest should be recorded separately, as it is noted separately on a US tax return. After you take out this accumulated interest, the number you are left with is your actual trading session's starting amount. Certainly, this could be confusing. So as you learn the craft, you may wish to run it by your accountant.

As you trade throughout the day, keep track of the gains and losses that are generated with each trade. This is easier with a smaller number of trades. You should also keep records of your trading for review purposes. If you are doing many trades each session or engaging in trades that are retained from session to session such as an FX carry trade, or longer-term accumulation of a position, there is another method of recording gains and losses.

This alternate method is perfectly acceptable as far as the IRS is concerned and is often used in CPA tax preparation offices where the client is a heavy trader. In this method, your day trading account's value at the beginning of the trading session is recorded. After your trades are made and your positions are opened and closed, you record your day trading account's ending balance.

Keep Track

Record additions to and subtractions from your day trading account properly. If you don't identify them on your record, you will lose track of what is profit and what are additions and subtractions of capital when you review your books during tax time.

The account's ending balance is subtracted from the beginning balance. The result is your net gain or loss for that trading session. This daily gain or loss is recorded in a separate book, labeled "Day Trading Gains/Losses per Session." Each session is recorded on a separate line, with the date, amount of gain or loss, and the words "day trading, various."

The combined records of your expenses, money spent on fixed assets, deposits into and out of your day trading accounts, and the record of your daily day trading gains and losses complete your record keeping. If you maintain your gains/losses record and your cash record, you are going a long way in keeping your day trading business's overall profits and losses easy to track and ready for any formal document preparation.

TRADING PROFITS, EXPENSES, AND TAXES

Tracking Net Income

Even though you will be recording your gains and losses from trading, what you are taxed on in the United States is your net income. This net income number is your net gains minus your expenses. This section will help you determine your net income from day trading.

COMMON EXPENSES

Normal expenses can vary but usually include the costs associated with the business use of your home, any mileage you might have incurred in the process of conducting business, the portion of utilities that are attributable to the operation of your day trading business, etc. Other expenses that can be used to reduce your overall net income include any subscription services, meals that were related to conducting business, and any travel (separate from your mileage amount) associated with your day trading business. Almost every cost associated with the establishment, upkeep, and conducting of your day trading business can be used as an expense on your income statement. This income statement usually records the gains and losses from the beginning of the year to the end of the year at the top of the page.

In a separate subheading, list the categories of expenses related to the direct production of your day trading gains. Some of the categories are related to the business use of your home. This is usually calculated by measuring the total square footage of the home that is used exclusively for business purposes (for instance, if you have one room you use as an office). This number is divided by the total square footage of the home. The resulting percentage is the amount of your rent expenses that can be assigned as a day trading business expense.

Guide to Business Deductions

There are usually a large amount of expenses that can be attributed to your day trading business. You might be able to find some excellent deductions if you consult one of the many guides to business expense deductions, including the Internal Revenue Service's (IRS) website: www.irs.gov/businesses.

That same percentage is also taken for any shared utilities expenses, such as electricity, heat, and water. Any repairs to the building are assigned to the business at this percentage, as are condominium maintenance expenses, such as condo and HOA fees. To figure what percentage of your home is used for business only, use the square footage of the room or rooms that serve as your office space and are used exclusively for business. There can be no dual-usage of these parts of the home.

PHONE LINES AND TECHNOLOGY

Another key factor in determining if you own an actual business is if you have a phone line for the business that is separate from your personal line. Having a landline in your home fulfills the requirement of having a separate home phone, and your cell phone can then be used as your business line. The IRS also looks favorably on a business that has its own separate post office box, since this shows that your endeavor is an actual business.

Other expenses include the depreciation of business equipment and software. While it is best to consult the tax code, generally any business funds that are spent on equipment are expensed and deducted over a period of several years. This is called depreciation expense, and the length of time and method of deduction can be determined by looking up the asset class in any number of tax guides that are available commercially.

The combination of your gains, losses, and related expenses result in what is called your net income. This net income number is the amount on which your business taxes will be based.

TAX PLANNING

In planning your taxes while considering your day trading profits, you can achieve the best results by matching your gaining trades with a losing trade of equal or near equal value. While you would naturally want to have more profitable trades than losing trades, matching as many trades as you can will lessen your tax bill.

For investors, this process can be done during the whole year, but when you are trading you have the advantage of matching up gains and losses with a shorter time frame, ideally with the net effect of reducing your net gains daily. You can match gains and losses on a weekly and monthly basis also. This matching is usually done by the closing out of positions that are on your books that are at a loss.

Normally, when building up a position for a long-term trade, you hold on to the position and continue to buy into the security as it got to lower points during the trade's holding time. Holding the security and buying in on the dips would normally be your strategy; you might even be glad that the security fell into a loss for a short time as this would offer an opportunity to buy even more of the security at a lower price.

If you were following the tax planning method, you would weed out some of your longer-term trades that are currently losing. You would close them out at a loss if you determined that they would not turn around soon. To take tax planning further, do this at least once a quarter, by closing out losing trades in the week before the end of the quarter.

CLEANING HOUSE

"Cleaning house" serves two purposes. First, get the losing, nonperforming trades off your books within a certain time limit (quarterly). The second purpose is to match your gains and losses at least once every quarter. This is important because if you are day trading full time, it is usually the custom to make quarterly estimated tax payments to the IRS. If you are matching your gains and losses, you will effectively be lowering your net income for each reportable quarter.

Your goal is to maximize profits, so you get rid of losing trades. These trades that are in a loss but are still on your books, whether you are waiting for them to "turn around" or are engaged in some other form of wishful thinking that they will somehow turn profitable. They are losing trades—close them out, free up the money, and at least get some tax benefits from them.

Another goal of tax planning is to accelerate your expenses so you can claim them sooner rather than later. This means that if you are planning a new computer purchase, software upgrade, or other investment in equipment, or thinking of incurring any other expenses, it makes sense to incur these expenses in an earlier reporting period rather than in a later period. That's because expenses reduce your overall net income, and this reduction of net income lowers your taxes. Remember that tax planning involves the reduction of your net gains by matching up your gains and losses.

This matching up has the overall effect of lowering the first part of your income statement, the net gains section, and should be done at least once a quarter. Matching up your gains and losses once a quarter allows you to pay lower quarterly estimated income taxes. It also weeds out the nonperforming trades on your books at least once every three months.

EXPAND YOUR KNOWLEDGE

Read, Study, and Develop

The average weekender looks at his club tennis match as exercise, but professional tennis players know that the real work is in the gym and on the practice court. Thus, you should set up a system to help you get ready for a day trading session, such as a checklist that you review before you start trading. Think both in the short and long term. In the short term, you may include your morning coffee or pre-trading exercise and what type of breakfast makes you the sharpest. In the long term, there is no substitute for a solid commitment to learning the craft. This section will discuss how to keep your knowledge, learning, and trading fresh and profitable as time goes on.

STUDY FIRST, TRADE LATER

This idea is applicable to any endeavor that requires a certain expertise level in a market environment. Whether you are a rare-coin dealer, a jewelry merchant, or a vintage motorcycles dealer, if you know your product and your market well enough, you will be able to spot many buying and selling opportunities and go far with your trading business.

The same is true for day traders. You should become so versed in your field that you can check the price of a future, ETF, currency pair, or stock at any time, from anywhere, and know if it is a buying or selling opportunity. Without knowing your market, you might find yourself missing a potential money-making trade. Study the market to become an expert, as if it's a subject to master before taking a test. This mastery takes a lot of time at first, but you will then be able to exploit your market knowledge in both offensive and defensive ways, protecting your capital and adding to your capital through profitable trades.

MASTERING YOUR SUBJECT

After your initial study of the terms of the market and day trading, study the economy in general and the sectors specifically. When you have a good grasp of how the market works, you are ready to trade. Start small at first, and try to make every trade a learning experience from spotting setups, to buy-in, to close.

Keep Up with Market News

If you are going to be away from day trading for a few days or even weeks, keep track of the market news by reading Investing.com on your smartphone, and get the app! If you don't stay tuned in to the market, information can pass you by, as the market can change quickly.

Invest time and effort in your education. Learning to day trade takes time and money and means studying setups and the market as often and as regularly as possible, including the commitment of capital and its exposure to trades. If you were to go to a top university and get an MBA in hopes of obtaining a job as a trader in one of the big investment banks, it would take several years of full-time study and $50,000 to $100,000+ in tuition. You can teach yourself for a lot less.

SEARCH FOR SETUPS

Two things are essential for a profitable day trading session: good setups and free capital to commit to the trades. If your money and margin are tied up in a grouping of positions that weren't thought out and were entered into haphazardly, you run the risk of tying up that capital and margin in losing positions. Your goal is to preserve your capital first and to have winning trades and to make money second; you should not trade for excitement or as an experiment. If you are going about day trading in the right way, you will have available cash and margin always waiting on the sidelines, always ready to enter good setups. Look for the best play of the day before you enter a trade.

THE DAY TRADING LEARNING CURVE

Learning about the economy, the markets, and how to day trade takes time. You can expect to spend several weeks or even months learning before you reach the point where you feel comfortable to make your first small trade. However, your real market knowledge will not set in until you have been actively day trading with actual money for several months. Even after six months you are still learning the subtleties of day trading and the goals that go with it, such as pyramiding, money management, and risk management.

Start your day trading off with a small amount of money and learn to day trade profitably before making additional deposits to your account. It will take you time to learn to read the markets, spot setups, and technically enter and exit positions properly. Give yourself time to learn the basics, as market conditions and setups usually develop slowly.

Simple Is Best

There is much information available out there for you to study and read to help you train for day trading. Just because someone or some company offers a complex system of trading that is difficult to learn does not mean you will have guaranteed results. The best systems are often the simplest and easiest to learn and the ones you can use successfully.

TAKE YOUR TIME

Budget your time realistically to train on more complex trades. For instance, you can give yourself three months of trading equities and ETFs before moving into leveraged ETFs with 2:1 or even 3:1 ratio. After getting comfortable with how a leveraged ETF reacts to the markets, you can begin day trading some of the bear ETFs that are available. After learning how to use equities and ETFs to learn the basics of order entry, leverage, and shorting the market, you can move on to day trading Forex, which will increase your available leverage ratio (from 10:1 to 500:1) and easily give you the ability to short currency pairs. On the other hand, after learning to read the market reports and analyze the fundamentals and technical aspects, you may want to move on to day trading some of the smaller-sized lots of futures, such as the e-mini S&P 500, and the e-mini commodity futures.

The overall goal is to give yourself enough time to have experiences winning and losing in the markets with a manageable amount of leverage and enough capital to feel the full emotions of day trading. Do this before moving into higher-leverage, higher-dollar accounts and riskier, faster-moving sectors. You should look at day trading as a long-term activity. With this in mind, take every precaution to ensure that you will be there to trade the next day with your account and wits intact.

Patience and Planning Are Virtues

It helps to craft your expectations carefully and then measure your progress slowly. Ask yourself where you'd like to be, not in two weeks, but in three to six months. Then set some reasonable goals and guidelines. For example, in three months you might be trading stocks with frequent profits while in six months you may shoot for starting to trade currencies. In nine months, it may make sense to consider commodities. And in a year, adding cryptocurrencies is a worthy goal. Write down your goal and how you're going to get there and check your progress toward the goal every two weeks. If you're not making progress, then you need to re-evaluate what you're doing and why you're not making progress.

ACKNOWLEDGMENTS

In the writing of this book, there was much help: I'd like to thank my editors at Simon & Schuster, Eileen Mullan and Jennifer Kristal, and the huge work they did to get this book to press. I'd like to thank the editorial board, because they liked the proposal and gave me enough time to write it. I'd also like to thank the best agent in the world, Grace Freedson, and Frank and Jean Kollar for helping to keep the lights on at JoeDuarteintheMoneyOptions .com. And last but not least, a heartfelt thanks to subscribers to JoeDuarteintheMoneyOptions.com, Buy Me a Coffee supporters (https://buymeacoffee.com/wsdetectivx), and my Smart Money Passport Substack (https://smartmoneypassport.substack.com) subscribers and followers.

INDEX

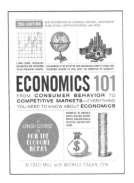